D0845182

Adjustment
to Work

The Century Psychology Series

Richard M. Elliott, Kenneth MacCorquodale,
Gardner Lindzey, Kenneth E. Clark

Editors

Adjustment to Work

A Psychological View of Man's Problems
in a Work-Oriented Society

Lloyd H. Lofquist
& René V. Dawis
University of Minnesota

APPLETON-CENTURY-CROFTS
EDUCATIONAL DIVISION
MEREDITH CORPORATION

New York

Copyright © 1969 by
MEREDITH CORPORATION
All rights reserved

This book, or parts thereof, must not be
used or reproduced in any manner without
written permission. For information address
the publisher, Appleton-Century-Crofts,
Educational Division, Meredith Corporation, 440 Park Avenue South, New York,
N. Y. 10016.

669-1

Library of Congress Card Number: 73-85886

PRINTED IN THE UNITED STATES OF AMERICA

390-57000-1

To our wives
Lillian and Lydia

Preface

The idea of this book had its beginnings in the development and publication of a Theory of Work Adjustment in 1964 with our colleague, Dr. George W. England. The theory itself resulted from several years of research activity in the area of work-adjustment outcomes. With the publication of the theory, the authors felt compelled to explicate the context for the theory, and to explore the possible applications of the theory to the problems of work in our society.

The Theory of Work Adjustment is a developing theory undergoing modification in the light of research findings. This will be evident to the reader who compares the 1964 publication with the 1968 revision which is presented in this book. It is hoped, however, that the current statement of the theory in the broader context of the discussion in this book will stimulate research and provide at least a tentative frame of reference for the teaching and practice of vocational psychology.

Our ideas are closely tied to our research commitments. The influence of the late Professor Donald G. Paterson had much to do with the shaping of the directions of our research and with our commitment to the development of a science of vocational psychology. In carrying out our research, we have been ably assisted by a talented and dedicated staff of research assistants. Special acknowledgment for assistance in shaping our ideas is given to Dr. George W. England and Dr. David J. Weiss, our current research director. We also appreciate the continuing stimulation and support of our colleagues in the Industrial Relations Center and in the Department of Psychology at the University of Minnesota. Special acknowledgment for assistance in the preparation of the manuscript is given to Mrs. Betty Adams.

The research carried out in the Work Adjustment Project continues to be supported, in large part, by the Rehabilitation Services Administration, Social and Rehabilitation Service, U.S. Department of Health, Education, and Welfare. Without this support it is unlikely that this program of research would have developed to its present level.

L. H. L.
R. V. D.

Contents

Adjustment
to Work

Prologue

Scene: small restaurant in a large industrial city

It is coffee-break time for the receiving room crew at McMaster's Merchandising warehouse. John Dow is the natural leader of the work group. He does as good a job as any and seems carefree all the time. To John the money is pretty good for a summer job, even though his father thinks the job is pretty low level. John has just finished high school with average grades. His best grades were in shop courses. He enjoys working with engines. John's father is a lawyer, as is his older brother. John knows that he is expected to go to college. But he has no idea what he'll take when he gets there.

Albert Fisher is the brains of the group. He seems forever to be reading books. He comes from a professional family but likes physical labor. He also wants his own money to spend on his many hobbies. Currently he is building a chemical laboratory and adding to his photographic equipment. Albert has always been an honor student without much effort. He seems enthusiastic about all his courses, from shop work to literature and art. Albert is also an accomplished trumpet player and was a member of his school's gymnastic team. Albert has one problem: he doesn't know what to do after graduation. He has thought of careers in physics, chemistry, art, or journalism, and just doesn't know what he'd like best. He hasn't mentioned college once.

Harold King talks about college all the time. He has been accepted by a local college. His parents are excited about the prospect of having a college-educated son; neither of them finished

1

high school. Ever since Harold's birth they have looked forward to his college years and have saved all they could for his education. Harold has been a hard-working student but he has only average grades. His high school counselor has told him that he might find college courses too difficult. He feels he can do college work and that anyone can finish college if he works hard enough. Harold believes strongly that everybody should go to college.

Benny Ray Jones is last to join the group. He is a Negro, and the newest employee. This is his fourteenth job in the three years since he left school at age 17. He has held jobs as dishwasher, loader, window washer, car washer, and stock room helper. On each job he was rated as an excellent employee, but the jobs didn't last. Benny Ray was a promising student in school, and had some dreams of college. This was all changed, however, when he had to become the breadwinner in the family. Now Benny Ray wonders whether he'll ever have his chance. He believes he can do college work but he didn't talk much with his school counselor and isn't sure what his life work should be. After his last job, he did go to an employment agency for counseling and placement. The counselor saw at once that Benny Ray had an excellent work record and placed him in work at the same level as his other jobs. Benny Ray is not happy about this job but he needs the money.

At a nearby table three employees of Tinker Engineering Design Company are also having a coffee break. They are talking about the fishing trip planned for next weekend. Ralph Edwardson, a draftsman, is the fisherman of the group. He likes his job and does it very well, but he lives for outdoor activities. He plans to continue as a draftsman until he can retire and perhaps operate a small resort.

Mr. Martin Merkel, the newly promoted office manager, looks forward to these fishing trips. He's not much of a fisherman but he needs to get away. Five years and three promotions ago he began as a draftsman. Because he was never really trained for management work, he finds the pressures hard to take. He likes the prestige of being an executive, and his family and friends expect him to rise even higher. When he is depressed, he thinks back to the time when, as a draftsman, he could see the finished products of his work. For Mr. Merkel, fishing provides brief periods of escape. Lately he seems to be thinking about fishing all the time.

John Rule, a mechanical engineer, likes fishing but he likes people even more. He thoroughly enjoys the company of Ralph and Martin. John is one of the best engineers in the firm and one of the most respected persons. To all who know him, John seems to have a very promising future with the company. But John himself is increasingly troubled with the routine, the detail, and the isolation of his work. He feels a strong need to be with people and has become a kind of unofficial father confessor to fellow employees such as Martin.

Shirley Simpson is everyone's favorite waitress. This is her third year on the job. She doesn't mind the hard work because she is paid well, but thinks maybe she could find a job in an office or as a salesperson. Shirley has had no specialized training; she finished high school. In high school she was more interested in boys than in preparing for a job. Marriage is uppermost in her thoughts but she would like to remain single for a few years yet. She likes this job because most of her customers are men.

Coffee-break time is over. It's Shirley's turn to take a break. She needs one, but it really is the dullest part of her day. Everyone else is at work.

1

The Meaning
of Work

WE LIVE IN A WORK-ORIENTED SOCIETY. IT IS EXPECTED THAT when a man reaches physical maturity he will engage in work. Larger and larger proportions of women are encouraged, even expected, to seek employment. Full employment is a national goal. Many of our social institutions are associated with work. If work is as highly valued in our society as it appears to be, it is necessary and desirable to study the relationship of man to his work, the problems a man faces in adjusting to work.

What does "work" mean to the individual? Typical definitions of work include: that activity in which he engages for pay, to make a living, or to earn money; the activity that occupies much of his waking day ("occupation"); the activity that utilizes his abilities or skills in some social or economic enterprise ("employment"); the activity which he feels called upon to do ("vocation"); or the activity which he contracts to do ("job"). These definitions do not bring out the full meaning of work to the individual. If work, as Roe (1956) points out, is truly the major focus of a person's activities and of his thoughts, then it assumes larger meaning than is implied in these definitions. If work provides a focal point for the development of one's way of life and if work is an important vehicle for one's total adjustment, then the meaning of work for the individual is much more than is contained in these definitions. Furthermore, the meaning of work cannot be understood properly unless it is viewed in the social context of work values held by the individual's society. Some understanding of these values should be facilitated by a brief review of the major thoughts men have had about work over the centuries (Tilgher, 1930).

Among the earliest recorded ideas (Hebrews, Greeks) about work are references to it as a curse, as a punishment, as activity not included as part of the good life, and as a necessary evil (necessary only to sustain life). Many of these ideas were religious in origin. Work took on meaning as a way of atonement for man's sins. Work was viewed as the means by which the kingdom of God might be fashioned on this earth. To these meanings of work, the early Christians added the concept of work as a means by which charity (that is, love of God through neighbor) could be expressed.

With the passing of the centuries, a distinction developed between work that was intellectual, spiritual, contemplative, and work that was manual, physical, exertive. The medieval universities, for instance, distinguished between the liberal arts and the servile arts (Pieper, 1952). The servile arts were undertaken for the satisfaction of basic human needs. The liberal arts could not be put at the disposal of such utilitarian, albeit necessary, ends. Performance of a liberal art could not, rightly speaking, be paid for. The honorarium was nothing more than a contribution given towards the liberal artist's living expenses. On the other hand, a wage meant payment earned for a servile art, that is, for a particular piece of work, and with no necessary reference to the cost-of-living needs of the worker.

To men of the middle ages work was a natural right and duty, the basis for society, the foundation for property, and the source of prosperity (Pieper, 1952). The notion of investment and interest (of making money without work) was to be condemned. Work was still a necessity, an obligation—but only insofar as it was necessary to maintain the individual and the group of which he was a part. Beyond this lay the higher life, the better life, the life of the intellect, the life of contemplation.

With the advent of Protestantism, new meanings of work evolved (Tilgher, 1930). Luther subscribed to the prevailing theory of work, but to this he added that all who could work should work, including the contemplatives and the ascetics. Furthermore, work of whatever station, high or low, was a way of serving God. For Luther, there was just one best way of serving God: doing most perfectly the work of one's occupation or profession.

But it was Calvin who brought radically new attitudes towards work. For Calvin, work alone sufficed to curb the evil bent of man. Therefore, all men—even the rich, the noble, and the ordained— needed to work. Work must be methodical, disciplined, rational, continuous—not intermittent or occasional. To this command to work ceaselessly, the ascetic Calvin added a command to renounce the fruits of work. Thus with Calvinism, the practice of invest- ment gained religious sanction and religious impetus. Max Weber asserts that it was the religious value of work and working, viewed as the highest means to asceticism, and as the strongest proof of religious faith, that must have been the strongest influence in shap- ing the capitalistic attitude (Weber, 1930). The stage was set for the age of capitalism.

At about this same time, a different viewpoint of work was emerging which expressed the spirit of the Renaissance. For men such as Leonardo da Vinci, work was the way by which man mastered nature. It was through work (man's toil, his arts and inventions) that he drew farther away from the animal and nearer to the divine. Man made for himself a second, higher nature of which he was the true god. As Tilgher points out, this was prob- ably the first time in history that the idea of valuing work for its own sake, of work as both its own end and its own purpose, gained widespread acceptance (Tilgher, 1930).

Work, then, has had at least three basic meanings for pre-in- dustrial men: 1) work was a hard necessity, painful and burden- some; 2) work was instrumental, a means towards ends, espe- cially religious ends; and 3) work was the creative act of man, therefore intrinsically good. It is probable that all three meanings of work have been present in various proportions at any period in man's history, but that one or another aspect received the greater emphasis, depending on the time, the place, and the man who was looking for the meaning of work.

With the Industrial Revolution and the advent of the machine, man became concerned with the relevance of work to his search for identity. Mechanization in work was seen as forcing man into the world of mass man or organization man. He was seen as reduced to a marginal, isolated, normless, insecure part of a man-machine system. In contemporary society, the advent of automation has accentuated these concerns and raised the specter of man being deprived of almost all of his work functions. With the "Second Industrial Revolution," man feels that the dehumanization of work reduces him to the humiliating status of machine-tender or machine-watcher. As machines perform an increasing number of work functions, society is faced with the question of what work will mean to man.

Another approach to the problem of determining the meaning of work is through the study of the effects of taking work out of people's lives. The unemployed and those who are retired provide two groups for such study.

Most studies on the unemployed are concerned with the economics of unemployment. A few deal with the psychological significance of unemployment to the unemployed. Bakke's studies (1934, 1940) on this problem are typical.

From interviews with unemployed individuals both in the United States and in England, Bakke concluded that loss of work leads to a series of demoralizing influences which strike a terrible blow against the unemployed worker's self-respect and self-confidence. The removal of furniture, the cutting down on food, foregoing the purchase of clothes, the lapse of insurance, foregoing social events —these consequences of unemployment have the total effect of removing the individual from, and denying him contact with, the world of which he was so recently so much a part. Bakke found that with prolonged unemployment the unemployed man tends towards the attitudes of pauperism and away from the desire to struggle back to his feet.

Unemployed men expressed the meaning of work in various ways. Some talked of a sense of being lost without the work to which they were accustomed. Others found enforced idleness to be unbearable, worse than cutting down on food and clothing. Many felt a sense of hopelessness, a sullen and despondent mood that mounted as the weeks without work went by. Unemployment was described as especially hard on the heads of families, who were bitter about their incapacity to perform traditional roles and functions, all the more so when they felt it was not their fault that they were unemployed. From Bakke's studies, there emerges a picture of the importance of work in the lives of these men.

Another group for whom the meaning of work comes sharply into focus is the group of workers who are coming to the end of their work careers. Several studies of work and retirement have been undertaken, of which those by Friedmann, Havighurst, and their University of Chicago associates (1954) serve as examples. Among the conclusions of this team of researchers were the following. Work does not have the same meaning for all individuals. Meanings vary as jobs and people vary. The significance of work, as interpreted by the worker himself, varies in two fundamental ways. First, it differs according to the particular recognition the person has made of the part which work has played in his life. Second, it differs according to the type of affective response the person has made to work. Yet some common threads do run through this diversity of meanings.

Friedmann et al. listed these common meanings of work to the workers they studied. Work is the means of maintaining a certain standard of living, a certain level of existence, and also of achieving some higher level or standard. Work is something to do, a way of filling the day or passing the time. Work is a source of self-respect, a way of achieving recognition or respect from others. Work defines one's identity, one's role in the society of which he is a part. Work provides the opportunity for association with others, for building friendships. Work allows for self-expression, provides the opportunity for creativity, for new experiences. Finally, work permits one to be of service to others.

One finding underscored by the Chicago group was that work has negative as well as positive meanings. The other side of the coin was expressed by some individuals as follows. Work does not provide enough rewards. The pay is rarely satisfactory. Work is dull, boring or exhausting, dangerous. Work reduces one's self-respect; it provides little prestige. Work forces on a person associations with people that he may not like. Work is uninteresting, distasteful. At work, one finds little opportunity for service to others, for self-expression, for creativity.

Other kinds of studies that help us to understand the meaning of work to the worker include studies of job satisfaction, of vocational interests, of vocational needs, and of work values. The many studies of job satisfaction in the literature indicate that only a small proportion of workers (about 15 percent) expressed dissatisfaction with their work, or more precisely, with their jobs (Robinson, Connors, and Robinson, 1964). The large majority of workers indicated satisfaction with their jobs. A listing of the reasons for job satisfaction included many of the meanings of work that have already been enumerated, such as security, opportunity for advancement, and good wages.

Studies of vocational interests tend to show similar meanings of work. From their review of vocational interest measurement, Darley and Hagenah (1955) concluded that for the large majority of workers, interest in work is primarily in terms of the subsistence income it provides, with other major human satisfactions being derived from sources extrinsic to work itself. For these workers, no definitive vocational interest patterns were found. It has since been demonstrated by Clark (1961), however, that interest patterns can be measured reliably for occupational groups below the professional and managerial classes. This suggests that work, even for lower-level workers, has satisfactions in addition to the survival value of the wages it provides.

Roe (1956) has stressed the importance that work has in the satisfaction of basic human needs. She feels that, in our society, work is the single situation most capable of providing some satisfaction for all levels of needs. Other studies indicate that work is important in need satisfaction and that there are differences in the needs being satisfied by different kinds of work (for example, Weiss, Dawis, England, & Lofquist (1964a, 1965). Studies of work values, such as that of Super (1962), may also yield information about the meaning of work.

It is apparent from this brief discussion of historical and research literature that modern man has inherited a cultural view of work and its meanings; that, in this view, work is central to man's development and total life adjustment; and that work provides a situation for satisfying needs. It is important next to explore the limits that man faces in seeking need satisfaction in work, and to examine how he can achieve adjustment in work.

References

Bakke, E. W. *The unemployed man.* New York: Dutton, 1934.

Bakke, E. W. *The unemployed worker.* New Haven: Yale University Press, 1940.

Clark, K. E. *Vocational interests of non-professional men.* Minneapolis: University of Minnesota Press, 1961.

Darley, J. G., and Hagenah, T. *Vocational interest measurement.* Minneapolis: University of Minnesota Press, 1955.

Friedmann, E. A., & Havighurst, R. J. *The meaning of work and retirement.* Chicago: University of Chicago Press, 1954.

Pieper, J. *Leisure, the basis of culture.* New York: Pantheon Books, 1952.

Robinson, H. A., Connors, R. P., & Robinson, A. Job satisfaction researches of 1963. *Personnel and Guidance Journal,* 1964, *43,* 360-366.

Roe, A. *The psychology of occupations.* New York: Wiley, 1956.

Super, D. E. The structure of work values in relation to status, achievement, interests, and adjustment. *Journal of Applied Psychology,* 1962, *42,* 231-239.

Tilgher, A. *Work: What it has meant to men through the ages.* New York: Harcourt, 1930.

Weber, M. *The Protestant ethic and the spirit of capitalism.* New York: Scribner, 1930.

Weiss, D. J., Dawis, R. V., England, G. W., & Lofquist, L. H. Construct validation studies of the Minnesota Importance Questionnaire. *Minnesota Studies in Vocational Rehabilitation,* XVIII, December, 1964.

Weiss, D. J., Dawis, R. V., England, G. W., & Lofquist, L. H. An inferential approach to occupational reinforcement. *Minnesota Studies in Vocational Rehabilitation,* XIX, December, 1965.

2

The Problems
Posed by Work

IN AMERICAN SOCIETY IT IS A MAXIM THAT EVERY INDIVIDUAL'S heritage includes the important freedom to choose his life work. There is a history of legislation designed to eliminate existing social barriers to the exercise of this freedom. Laws to insure equal employment opportunities and to provide economic opportunities are recent examples of this type of legislation.

While the individual's freedom to choose his work is unchallenged as a basic right, it is nevertheless constrained by a number of complex forces. A person from another culture would probably see these forces as emanating from our American way of life. He would observe, for example, that we exhort our young people to "hitch your wagon to a star," to "grow up to be president," or to be some kind of prestigious person such as a scientist, movie star, or professional athlete. Many of the heroes that are held up to young people represent "self-made," "rags to riches," "log cabin to the White House," "sandlot to the big league" success stories. It would also be apparent to our visitor that although these "success figures" represent a minute portion of the total number of successful workers in our society, we have built powerful stereotypes of success-in-work on them. Our visitor might question the appropriateness of our success models. Consequently, he might also remark that while the individual in American society may be free to choose his work, he is expected to choose well.

There are other constraints on freedom of work choice which our visitor might miss. The social scientists would observe pressures on the individual which stem from his social class membership. Membership in a social class implies certain limits on work-choice opportunities. The "accidents" of birth which place an individual in a sex group, race group, and/or socioeconomic status group, determine to some degree the kinds of work that he might consider for a career. In spite of progressive national policies and legislation to insure freedom of choice, the fact is that class membership factors still operate to restrict work choice (Hewer & Neubeck, 1962).

The social scientist would also see the role of smaller social groups, such as the family and the peer group, in restricting the field of work choices. Pressures to follow family work traditions, to avoid the "mistakes" of the father, to "keep the gang together," to do as well as brother, a neighbor, or a friend, are typical examples of the forces exerted by small groups.

In addition, there are constraints on freedom of choice that are "built into" each individual who is in the process of choosing his life work. He has a unique heredity and a unique history of experiencing and reacting to the many pressures exerted by his society, social class, family, and peer group. To the behavioral scientist each individual has a unique personality which places certain constraints on the range of choices that he will consider. Even members of the same social class, family, or peer group, will consider different choices because of their unique personalities.

One set of work-related problems, then, is centered on the constraints and/or pressures surrounding the important freedom of an individual to choose his life work. What appears to be freedom of choice is in reality a process strongly influenced by our national way of life, by the individual's social class membership, and by the unique personality that the individual possesses. There are a number of other problems in choosing, entering, and continuing at work that make these difficult tasks for an individual.

An individual is subjected to pressures to enter into work as he approaches physical maturity, even though the reasons are not always evident to him. He may find himself suddenly expected to assume his own economic responsibilities. Since, in many cases, this has not been required in the past, the individual may find it difficult to understand why he has now acquired social and economic responsibilities. These pressures on the maturing individual are combined with other cultural values which exalt work. There are widely held beliefs in our culture (see Chapter 1): that it is good to work for the sake of working; that idleness is not to be condoned and in fact is injurious to a person's well-being; that security is of paramount importance and is tied in closely with work and with having work skills; that everyone should be a productive member of society, contributing his share to the common good; and that one should use his innate abilities in productive work. These cultural values, present since childhood, take on personal significance for the maturing adolescent.

As the individual responds to these pressures he begins to explore work opportunities. His curiosity may lead him to explore the kinds of jobs that exist and their characteristics, requirements, and availability. He is likely to find that the world of work is very complex and that job exploration is both time-consuming and frustrating.

The complexities of the world of work are illustrated by a number of labor market realities. There are a vast number of occupations in our society. For example, the latest edition of the *Dictionary of Occupational Titles* (1965) lists over 35,000 occupational titles for over 21,000 separately defined occupations. Supplements to this publication will provide additional titles. Furthermore, these titles represent national descriptions which do not reflect the many local variations in job descriptions for a single occupational title. It is virtually impossible for an individual to secure and evaluate the necessary occupational information to choose from among this impressive array of jobs. Even if he limits himself to his local labor market, the individual will find it a formidable task to explore the large number of occupations and the relevant occupational information.

When an individual seeks job openings for specific occupations, he is faced with additional complicating factors resulting from the intricate workings of the labor market (Wolfbein, 1964). Change is the normal condition in the labor market. Very large numbers of people move in and out of the labor market, or from job to job, each day. It is difficult for any individual to keep abreast of daily changes and, more specifically, to know where job openings can be found, or to predict where job openings will be likely to exist at some future date.

It is true that a federal-state system of employment services exists and that provision has been made in this system both for the centralization of occupational and labor market information and for the location of job openings, especially at the middle and lower occupational levels. However, studies (Parnes, 1954; Reynolds, 1951) indicate that a relatively small number of persons use the services either of these public agencies, or of private employment agencies, to secure work. It appears that most individuals find work through information given by relatives and friends. Since these informants themselves are likely to be fairly naïve about occupational information, it follows that most persons choose their jobs from among a very limited number of job possibilities and on the basis of restricted occupational information.

It is also true that, in recent years, the number of high school counselors available to assist students in planning their educational and vocational careers has increased markedly. Many of these counselors make use of occupational information. There is, however, only limited integration of the activities of secondary school guidance counselors with the federal-state employment service programs (Hoyt & Loughary, 1958). It is also likely that vocational guidance in the high schools emphasizes the higher-level and professional occupations, which will be inappropriate for a large number of high school students.

It is apparent that at the present time the employment services and the secondary school guidance programs do not meet the needs of most individuals about to begin work. Furthermore, it is ironic that vocational counseling services that utilize professionally trained counselors and that give consideration to the full range of occupations are routinely available only to special groups such as disabled persons and social agency clients. The "normal" individual is left to his own devices. He makes his work choices in the absence of adequate occupational counseling and information.

If a young person who is about to enter the labor market is curious about the kinds of jobs that are most suitable for him, he will encounter another problem related to work choice, namely the problem of knowing himself in educational and work-related terms. In addition to knowing approximately what he can do, the individual should have a rather clear idea of what conditions he would find satisfying in work. In short, the individual requires knowledge of his unique characteristics as they relate to work.

The point has already been made that each individual has a unique personality which places certain constraints on the range of occupational choices that he will consider. People differ. Furthermore, these individual differences are not limited to preferences (for work or other activities) but are found for skills, abilities, physical characteristics, and, for that matter, for any measurable trait.

Biochemical Individuality, by Williams (1956), dramatically illustrates the existence of such individual differences where they are not ordinarily thought to exist. The author points out that there are large variations in the size, shape, and location of human organs (heart, stomach, colon, liver, and so forth) of normal individuals. It thus becomes obvious that the schematic representation of a human heart, for example, is really a composite of the many individual variations in normal hearts. An individual can be normal even though his heart is anatomically different from this composite.

People differ also in personality characteristics. For example, they differ in what they can do, not ordinarily on the basis of whether or not they have an ability, but rather in terms of how much of each kind of ability they have. They also differ in their preferences for different kinds of conditions.

In order to know his unique personality an individual must know the psychological traits that are relevant and his standing on each of them. Notwithstanding the protests of those writers who abhor psychological tests (such as Gross, 1962; Wernick, 1956), these instruments of the behavioral scientist provide the best available means for the description of psychological traits and of an individual's unique personality. It is not generally true that the individual who has in these times taken several psychological tests, has been pigeon-holed with regard to his occupational possibilities, as is claimed by those who decry the "brain watchers" or the "psychometrician kings." This belief stems from a misconception of the proper use of psychological tests. Tests may be used as aids in choosing occupations. They contribute to predictions of success or failure, and in this sense provide an individual with a means of arriving at better-informed choices.

Although an individual goes through work-relevant experiences and takes various psychological tests as he progresses through school, the relevance of his experiences to his work is rarely called to his attention, and the tests he takes are given for reasons not specifically or directly related to work. In other words, he develops personality traits that have relevance for work, but he ordinarily has little organized knowledge of their nature and amount.

It is not usually true that "the individual knows himself best" when occupational choices are involved. He may know the nature and amount of some of his abilities, but he needs to know his unique total personality structure as it can be described by the pattern of his standing on several traits in comparison with other individuals, and the relevance of his pattern for different occupational possibilities. He needs the help of a professional person trained in these matters—for example, a vocational counselor.

At the present state of knowledge, vocational counselors have available to them instruments, techniques, and information about educational and occupational requirements that make it possible to help the individual make better-informed judgments about occupational possibilities. When vocational counselors are available to individuals, they can be helpful in resolving some of the problems of vocational choice. Unfortunately, the help that can currently be given is restricted to a limited number of predictions related largely to success in education and/or training for an occupation. Many of the prediction studies are designed to predict grade-point averages for specific course studies or specific occupational training programs, but do not relate clearly to a longer-term objective such as career success. This state of affairs appears to have resulted from an overemphasis on purely educational and training goals, arrested progress in the development of vocational psychology, and a paucity of interest in the development of theories of work. What is needed is a psychology of work.

The many problems that surround work (vocational choice, job finding, and work adjustment), which result from its central position in human activity, call for a systematic study of human behavior as it relates to work. There is a need to provide more substantial underpinnings for the practice of vocational counseling. We must become able to describe individuals more completely in work-relevant terms. We must become able to describe occupations more completely and in terms that relate to the individual and his work-relevant problems. We need systematic ways of relating characteristics of individuals to information about occupations. We must provide vocational counselors with techniques that will enable them to make predictions concerning such matters as occupational success, job satisfaction, and work adjustment. In short, we need to accelerate activity in vocational psychology. Brayfield (1961) is even more emphatic, and points to the necessity for placing the highest priority on the development of a science of vocational psychology that will provide the basis for the practice of vocational counseling.

Such a psychology of work requires investigation of psychological principles as they operate in work behavior. It requires the application of psychological concepts to understanding the nature and eventual solution of work problems. A theoretical framework is needed to enable us to conceptualize the development of the individual as a person ready for work, the development of the individual as a working person, the individual's adjustment to work, and the effects of having chosen certain occupations. In addition, the theoretical framework should enable us to conceptualize work in such a way that we can account for the impact of physical and/or social trauma and changes, such as disability, displacement by automation, and retirement.

The objectives in establishing a psychology of work should include the development of research hypotheses and the testing of these in an empirical manner. With the accumulation of facts, a science of vocational behavior can be built on solid foundations. More effective practices for professional vocational counselors should emerge from such a science.

This plea to establish a psychology of work in a revitalized vocational psychology is not intended to minimize the many advances that have been made in conceptualizing the counseling process and in developing its techniques, for example, in interviewing and psychological testing. Rather, it is intended to focus attention on the need of vocational counselors for data, techniques, and principles that will enable them to function as experts in the understanding of problems of work choice and work adjustment. Obviously, even with such a psychology of work at his disposal, the vocational counselor will still need all the information and skill he can muster in order to communicate effectively with his counselees.

Our focus in the next Chapter is on a psychological description of the work personality. The concept of the work personality provides the basis for the development of a theory of work adjustment in Chapter 5. It is hoped that this theory will contribute to the psychology of work.

References

Brayfield, A. H. Vocational counseling today. In Williamson, E. G. (Ed.), *Vocational counseling: A reappraisal in honor of Donald G. Paterson*. Minneapolis: University of Minnesota Press, 1961.

Gross, M. L. *The brain watchers*. New York: Random House, Inc., 1962.

Hewer, V. H., & Neubeck, G. Occupations of fathers and mothers of entering University of Minnesota freshmen, fall, 1959. *Personnel and Guidance Journal,* 1962, *40,* 622–627.

Hoyt, K. B., & Loughary, J. W. Acquaintance with, and use of referral sources by Iowa secondary school counselors. *Personnel and Guidance Journal,* 1958, *36,* 388–391.

Parnes, H. S. *Research on labor mobility*. New York: Social Science Research Council, 1954.

Reynolds, L. G. *The structure of labor markets*. New York: Harper, 1951.

U.S. Department of Labor, Bureau of Employment Security. *Dictionary of occupational titles*. Washington: U.S. Government Printing Office, 1965.

Wernick, R. *They've got your number*. New York: Norton, 1956.

Williams, R. G. *Biochemical individuality, the basis for the genotrophic concept*. New York: Wiley, 1956.

Wolfbein, S. L. *Employment and unemployment in the United States*. Chicago: Science Research Associates, 1964.

3

The Work
Personality

IN ONE APPROACH TO THE UNDERSTANDING OF HUMAN BEHAVIOR, psychologists view the individual as a responding organism. He can be observed to respond in a variety of ways. He responds to different environmental conditions, that is, to sets of stimuli, or to stimulus conditions. He responds differently at different times to what appear to be similar stimulus conditions. Some of his responses appear to be *reactions to* his environment. Other responses appear to be *actions on* the environment.

The individual has been observed to respond to different kinds of stimulation (Hooker, 1936) even before birth. At this stage, responding is limited to such behavior as movement. In the earliest years of development, behavior consists mainly of reactions to the environment. As the individual develops, actions on the environment increase in number, the individual becomes increasingly capable of differential responding, and his response repertoire for coping with the environment expands. He develops a variety of sensorimotor skills and soon becomes able to communicate with other individuals. His communication skills become more refined, more efficient, and more complex when he begins to talk.

As a responding and communicating organism the individual is now able not only to respond but also to report his experiences with responding. He can report on his experience with the stimulus conditions of his environment, and on how he responded. He can compare stimulus conditions and his responses from one environment to another. Since he can report on his past experiences, he exhibits what is called memory. Memory provides points of reference against which he compares present experience. Since each individual is unique at birth with respect to response potentials, and since no two environmental stimulus conditions will be exactly alike, the individual's memory provides a unique reference system for *evaluating* his present experiences. He reports on stimulus conditions and modes of response as they are viewed in the context of his past experience. His reports will, however, be uniquely his. They may not agree with reports by other individuals of his responses and of the stimulus conditions in which they occurred.

An individual's experiences with stimulus conditions in an environment, and with various modes of responding, can also be observed and described by another individual. The outside observer sees the responding that accompanies specific stimulus conditions and the changes in responding associated with changes in stimulus conditions. These observations permit the observer to make inferences regarding an individual's experiences. They also allow him to describe the development of an individual's response repertoire.

An individual's report of his experiences with responding may differ, sometimes markedly, from the report of another individual who is observing him. This suggests the desirability of considering both kinds of reports when describing an individual's behavior. Furthermore, reports made by different observers about an individual's behavior may differ in various degrees. Each other person observing an individual's behavior has his own unique memory to provide reference points for his observations and for his reporting of observed responses. He may, then, report observations that are as much reflections of his own experiences as they are assessments of the responses of the individual under observation. To increase the reliability of these observations, and to minimize the subjectivity of independent observers, it is necessary to use several observers and to introduce communicable standards for observation. Observations of this kind provide more objective reference points with which an individual's report of his behavior can be compared.

In organized societies, an individual's behavior is viewed by others largely in terms of the social norms or the social standards of behavior that have developed from the society's collective experience. In effect, society has written prescriptions for acceptable behavior for a variety of environmental settings, such as the family, the church, the school, and the work setting. These prescriptions are modified with the passage of time. In a stable society, social norms remain relatively fixed. Patterns of acceptable behavior are well defined. Social institutions are set up to administer the social norms and to promote the development of individual behavior along the lines of the prescribed patterns. All of the responses of a developing individual are made in this context.

To summarize, an individual's reports of his behavior are made in the contexts of both his memory and his knowledge of social standards. The independent observer's report of the individual's behavior, if made in the context of communicable standards for observation, may differ from the self-report. There are, then, at least two major independent sources of data available for the description of an individual's behavior: the report of the individual himself, and the report of other persons. An understanding of an individual's behavior must utilize both sources of data. One source communicates from a private, or more subjective, frame of reference, the other from a public, or more objective, view of behavior. These two sources of data can be used to describe a *stable characterization* of the individual as a responding organism, or what is called an individual's *personality*.

In observing an individual's behavior, one can identify recurring response sequences. These recurring response sequences tend to become modified and more refined with repetition. They are called *skills*. Over time an individual develops a large repertoire of skills. While each individual's repertoire is unique, it is feasible to identify similar response sequences in the repertoires of several individuals. This identification of a common skill for several individuals permits the definition of a *skill dimension*. A skill dimension is defined in terms of such characteristics as: level of difficulty, economy of effort, and efficiency. A skill dimension reflects individual differences in a specific skill; people can be ranked along such a dimension in terms of how skillful they are.

The number of skill dimensions is, however, extremely large. It is cumbersome to describe individual responding in terms of many skill dimensions. A more succinct system of description is feasible through the application of modern mathematical methods. Using factor analysis (Harman, 1960) it is possible to identify a smaller number of more basic dimensions that underlie the several skill dimensions. These more basic dimensions represent common elements in skill dimensions, and are called *ability dimensions*. Obviously, there are fewer ability dimensions than skill dimensions. It is more feasible, therefore, in terms of both economy of time and comprehensiveness of scope, to describe individual behavior in terms of ability dimensions.

Even when ability dimensions are defined in the above manner, the problem of measuring the full range of an individual's abilities remains a formidable task. Each dimension will require a specific measure, and obviously there are many different ways of constructing a measure for an ability dimension. Such measures are commonly known as psychological tests. Psychological tests can be constructed to measure factor-analytically-derived ability dimensions. (See, for example, French, 1954.) Theoretically, any skill can be described by making reference to the measurements obtained by administering these psychological tests.

Measurements of abilities taken at different points in the course of an individual's development will show change. An individual's abilities are characterized as stable when repeated measurements show little change.

Measured ability is not the same as the utilization of ability. Utilization requires the appropriate stimulus conditions. In his lifetime an individual experiences a tremendous variety of stimulus conditions. As he develops he responds in many different stimulus situations. As similar stimulus conditions are encountered by an individual, he can report similarities not only in terms of describing the stimulus conditions and his response, but also in terms of his evaluation of responding under these conditions. In other words, he develops his own norms for evaluating stimulus conditions in which he may respond (usually in terms of whether or not they are satisfying to him). He describes these norms as his *preferences* for stimulus conditions. These (individual) norms are separate from but analogous to society's norms for individual behavior (that is, the behavior that "satisfies" society).

An outside observer can also describe stimulus conditions under which a person responds, and can compare responding under different stimulus conditions. However, in order to infer the individual's norms for evaluating stimulus conditions, an observer would have to observe and record an individual's total history from birth. Since this continuous observation is not feasible the observer gains information about any individual's norms or preferences for stimulus conditions by observing response in a defined stimulus situation or by obtaining the individual's stated preferences.

When a set of stimulus conditions is observed to be consistently associated with continued responding we refer to the stimulus conditions as *reinforcers* and to the maintenance or increase of responding as *reinforcement*. Different reinforcers maintain, or reinforce, responding at different frequency levels. In other words, different reinforcers have different *reinforcement values* for an individual. In addition, the same reinforcer may have different reinforcement values for different individuals.

An individual's norms, or preferences, for stimulus conditions reflect the different reinforcement values of the stimulus conditions that he has experienced. This experience with different reinforcers is organized by the individual into a pattern of preferences.

An observer can describe a given set of stimulus conditions in terms of different reinforcement values that appear to be associated with different classes of response for an individual. He can also describe a set of stimulus conditions in terms of different reinforcement values associated with the same class of responses for different individuals. He can state the probability of responding by an individual under different stimulus conditions. He can do this without reference to the individual's description of his preferences for stimulus conditions.

If the observer states the probability of an individual's responding under different stimulus conditions by using that individual's report of his preferences for stimulus conditions, he must take into account the distinction between observed reinforcement values and reinforcement values as reported by the individual. It is useful to speak of reinforcement values that are *actual* (experienced by the individual), *stated* (reported by the individual), and *observed* (reported by an observer). Stated reinforcement values may differ from observed values; actual values are inferred from stated and/or observed values. Reinforcement values are associated with the probability of the individual's responding under specified stimulus conditions and have, therefore, utility for predicting response under specified stimulus conditions.

Since reinforcement values for the same stimulus condition will differ for different individuals it is possible to speak of a *reinforcement-value dimension* for each stimulus condition. It is obvious that the description of all stimulus conditions in these terms is unrealistic. It is necessary, then, to consider the possibility of classifying these dimensions within a less elaborate system. This can be achieved by using factor-analytic procedures to identify a smaller number of more basic dimensions that underlie the many reinforcement-value dimensions. These more basic dimensions represent common elements in several reinforcement-value dimensions. Because these basic dimensions represent preferences for stimulus conditions in which responding is usually associated with satisfaction they may be designated as *need* dimensions. These need dimensions represent reported or observed similarities in the reinforcement values of stimulus conditions. For example, stated or observed preferences for responding in large group situations such as a family reunion, a church social event, a company picnic, or a political rally, might be described in terms of a need dimension which appropriately describes all of the separate stimulus situations, such as the need for affiliation, rather than as separate needs for each situation.

It should be noted that the term *need* is used here to designate the reinforcement values of stimulus conditions. This differs from common usage in which this term is used to denote some particular state of deprivation. While deprivation may serve to increase the reinforcement value of stimulus conditions, the significant *psychological* fact is the magnitude of the reinforcement value regardless of its derivation. For this reason, such needs can be thought of as *psychological needs*. The needs discussed in this book are these psychological needs.

Psychological needs can be measured in at least two ways. Questionnaires (inventories, surveys) can be used to obtain individuals' *reported* preferences for stimulus conditions. Observers can judge the relative reinforcement values of some stimulus conditions for individuals. Psychological needs, whether reported or observed, are said to be stable when successive measurements show little change. Measurements on a set of psychological need dimensions become, for most people, relatively stable as the individual reaches physical maturity. There are, of course, individual differences in the point in time when the set of needs becomes stable.

This concept of need stability is based on the observation that for the most part individuals live out their lives in relatively stable environments where similar stimulus conditions are experienced from day to day. With marked changes in environment, some change in an individual's psychological needs may result. Only in extremely rare instances will much change be expected if the marked environmental change occurs after psychological maturity, that is, after the set of needs has become relatively stable.

In the preceding paragraphs the point has been made that it is more feasible to describe an individual's personality in terms of abilities and needs rather than at the conceptual level of skills and reinforcement values. It is also expected that measurements of abilities and needs should be more stable. For these reasons the discussion that follows will be at the level of abilities and needs.

A set of complex interrelationships may be observed between abilities and needs. For example, an ability may be associated with one or several needs. Similarly, a need may be associated with one or several abilities. Within this set of complex interrelationships *competition* (representing equivalence) or *prepotency* (representing hierarchical ordering) may operate for needs in relation to abilities, or for abilities in relation to needs. What is termed *conflict* occurs when there is competition between incompatible needs in relation to an ability or between incompatible abilities in relation to a need. For example, the need for affiliation may conflict with the need for achievement when the people who are reinforcing to the individual will not permit full utilization of his abilities; or the utilization of high verbal ability and high motor ability may produce conflict when an individual with a strong ability-utilization need finds himself in a work setting with a choice of jobs that permit successful performance by using either ability but not both. Inasmuch as most individuals exhibit few enduring conflicts and behave in relatively integrated fashion in most situations, need-ability relationships are felt to be organized largely on the basis of the hierarchical ordering, or prepotency, existing for an individual's needs as well as his abilities.

One common way in which an individual expresses his own ability-need relationships is to state preferences for various kinds of activities. These preferences appear to sample, in rough fashion, a number of classes of activity which have occurred in the experience of the individual. For example, when asked about his favorite activities, he may express preferences for bowling, playing golf, reading biographies, and tinkering with machines. These preferences may be termed *expressed* or *stated interests*. When the behavioral scientist wishes to assure an orderly and comprehensive sampling of activity preferences likely to have occurred in the experience of most people (so that comparisons can be made among people) he provides a structure within which each individual expresses his activity preferences in the form of an interest inventory. Activity preferences obtained in this way may be termed the individual's *measured interests*. These measured interests are stated interests but, because of the structure provided, they yield a better sampling of classes of activity preferences and a more comprehensive statement of an individual's total set of preferences for activities. The standard structure and conditions under which activity preferences are reported also make it possible to establish the consistency of measurement, or reliability, and to compare measured activity preferences for different individuals and groups.

An individual's ability-need relationships may also be observed and continuously recorded in a systematic fashion. Records of participation in defined activities may be compiled by observers. The defined activities with which we are concerned are those for which an alternative to participation was available, in other words, ones in which the individual was not forced to participate. The observers may include such persons as the individual's teachers, employers, colleagues, friends, public officials, or behavioral scientists conducting a longitudinal study. These evidences of participation in activities may be termed *exhibited interests*. Where there is agreement between measured interests and exhibited interests, one might speak of *validated interests*.

Interests are seen, then, as deriving from the interaction of needs and abilities (or, more basically, from the interaction of reinforcement values and skills). The stability of interests is contingent upon the stabilization of an individual's set of needs and abilities (that is, upon his reaching psychological maturity) and can be observed in most people to occur with the attainment of physical maturity.

Another common way in which an individual expresses ability-need relationships is to state the likelihood of his behaving in particular ways. Such statements may be termed *expressed* or *stated personality descriptions*. When these descriptions are made within the framework of a psychometric instrument (usually an inventory) constructed to sample a broad range of human behaviors in systematic fashion (for example, according to some theoretical orientation), one may speak of *measured personality descriptions*.

It is also possible to base personality descriptions on records compiled by observers. These evidences of ability-need relationships may be termed *descriptions of exhibited personality*. When the descriptions of exhibited personality agree with measured personality descriptions, one might speak of *validated personality descriptions*.

Personality description, whether stated, measured, or observed, may also be based on an individual's ranking with reference to other people on a *personality characteristic*. Personality characteristics represent classes of behavior. Such descriptions are commonly reported as ratings of an individual on such personality dimensions as aggression, surgency, and dependency.

In the present state of psychometric technology, measures of interests and of personality description are valuable tools for inferring the ability-need relationships of the individual. It is felt, however, that the complex interrelationships between abilities and needs can be better understood if one starts directly with ability and need measurements. This approach obviously requires a greatly improved technology. The viewpoint presented in this book anticipates advances in technology and focuses on abilities and needs as major personality variables.

The individual's set of abilities, his set of needs, and the interaction of his abilities and needs constitute the *structure of his personality*. When measurements of these abilities and needs are stable, personality structure is said to be stable. Personality structure, however, does not describe the personality in action. When we consider how an individual utilizes his abilities and seeks to satisfy his needs, we require concepts in addition to those defining personality structure. These concepts are of two kinds: one characterizes the style of responding (for example, speed of responding), the other describes the style of reacting to stimulus conditions (for example, tolerance for delay of reinforcement). The first concept relates to abilities, the second to needs. These concepts taken together describe what may be called *personality style*. Personality structure and personality style are both required to describe the personality in action.

Much of the work in personality description has focused on personality structure. Less attention has been given to personality style. Measured personality descriptions (see page 32) are, in part, attempts to describe personality style. They rely, however, on *reports* of style rather than on actual data on style. Data on style should be based on prolonged and continuous observation of the personality in action. Cumulative records of the type kept in school probably come closest to approaching the accumulation of the kind of data on personality style that is needed. In much the same way as personality structure can be observed to exhibit stability, personality style can be said to be stable when its measurement shows little change.

When the behavioral scientist is concerned with the decription of personality as it contributes to the understanding of *work behavior,* he limits himself to those abilities and needs that are most *relevant,* and describes the structure and style of the individual's unique *work personality*.

From a practical standpoint, the determination of the *relevant* abilities and needs in a work personality is made by both the employer and the employee. The employer specifies the behavior required in the achievement of the work organization's goals. He also determines the stimulus conditions in which this behavior will take place, and he sets up the reinforcements intended to stimulate and maintain appropriate behavior. We are aware of the fact that employer latitude in making these determinations is limited by the actions of government, organized labor, and competing work organizations.

In a very real sense the employee also affects employer specifications of the work environment and the work requirements. Employee satisfaction influences acceptance of employer requirements and the work environment. The employee may accept, change, or reject the employer's specifications. In order to recruit and hold workers, the employer must attend to employee satisfaction.

In this manner, employer and employee jointly determine the

abilities and needs that are relevant in the work setting and these abilities and needs describe the structure of the work personality.

Having defined the variables relevant to the description of the work personality, discussion of the development of the work personality is required to provide a context for conceptualizing work adjustment.

In discussing the development of the work personality we start with the assumption that each individual has his unique potentialities for responding. The limits of these potentialities with respect to variety (in kind), range (in number), and complexity (in interacting combinations) are presumably determined by heredity. Responding by an individual is contingent on appropriate potentialities for response, and an environment that permits and/or stimulates responding. An individual's potentialities are inferred from his normative status as a member of a biological class (with respect to species and sex) and an age group (with respect to developmental or maturational level), and from his behavior (including his response to stimulus conditions contrived to explore the limits of his response capabilities, such as psychological tests).

The regular appearance of particular response capabilities at certain points in the life histories of several individuals allows the observer to describe an individual in terms of stages of behavior development. The earliest responses appear in the maintenance of physiological functioning, or result from direct stimulation. Later responses do not appear to be directly related to the maintenance of physiological functioning or to direct stimulation, but rather may be described as attempts by the individual to explore and to "act on" his environment. Responses are no longer limited to specific reactions to specific stimulation (elicited responses) but occur under varying conditions of stimulation (emitted responses).

There appear to be three principal stages of behavior development. They can be described as: a *differentiation stage* in which the individual is observed to explore, develop, and expand his response capabilities in terms of variety, range, and complexity (Garrett, 1946); a *period of stability* characterized by the crystallization and maintenance of a response repertoire; and a *stage of decline* in which response capabilities are affected by physiological changes associated with aging.

All responding obviously takes place in environmental settings.

Most of it takes place in social environments. During the differentiation stage much of it takes place in educational environments. During the stability period much of it takes place in work environments. In the course of his development an individual experiences a variety of reinforcers. Most of these reinforcers are those typically available in predominantly social and educational environments.

It is possible to describe the developing personality in terms of abilities and needs at different points in the differentiation stage. At very early ages we observe principally the development of motor abilities and the dominance of physiological needs. As the individual achieves increased mastery of his physical environment and as he learns to communicate with and to interact with other individuals he exhibits a large variety of abilities and needs. There may be periods in the differentiation stage of behavior development when the number of abilities and needs increases or changes very rapidly (for example, when a child starts school or when he reaches puberty). These periods of sudden change are typically associated with marked changes in physical maturation and/or environmental stimulation.

With physical maturity the individual is typically observed to exhibit relatively crystallized and stable abilities and needs. *Crystallization* refers to the retention of a particular set of abilities and needs in the personality structure. *Stabilization* refers to the maintenance of abilities and needs at relatively constant levels of strength and hierarchical ordering.

The process of crystallization and stabilization of both abilities and needs is accompanied by the development of a unique personality style. With a crystallized and stable personality structure and style the individual may be described as having a fully developed or mature personality. It is then possible to describe this mature personality in terms of measured abilities and needs. For most people, physical and psychological maturity are achieved at about the same time (Anastasi, 1958; Tyler, 1965). It is also at this time that most people begin their work experience.

With work experience, the individual encounters some new stimulus conditions and may develop some new abilities. In the initial period of work experience, and with changes to new work environments, some change may be observed in an individual's abilities and needs. The individual also may maintain some abilities and needs at high strength levels even though they are not involved in the work experience. Many abilities and needs are relevant to work, that is, they are required and reinforced by it; others are related to non-work activity. The work personality is defined in terms of those abilities and needs of the individual that have relevance for work.

References

Anastasi, A. *Differential psychology.* (3rd ed.) New York: Macmillan, 1958.

French, J. W. *Manual for kit of selected tests for reference aptitude and achievement factors.* Princeton, New Jersey: Educational Testing Service, 1954.

Garrett, H. E. A developmental theory of intelligence. *American Psychologist,* 1946, *1,* 372-378.

Harman, H. H. *Modern factor analysis.* Chicago: University of Chicago Press, 1960.

Hooker, D. Early fetal activities in mammals. *Yale Journal of Biology and Medicine,* 1936, *8,* 579-602.

Tyler, L. *The psychology of human differences.* (3rd ed.) New York: Appleton-Century-Crofts, Inc., 1965.

4

The Work
Environment

THE WORK ENVIRONMENT IS THE SETTING IN WHICH WORK BE-
havior takes place. This setting has traditionally been described
from the point of view of the employer. For example, the work environment is usually described in such terms as work to be performed, tools and materials used, job title, and rate of compensation. This type of description is based on an economic view of
work in which the individual worker is seen largely as one of the
factors in production. This is illustrated by the typical approaches
to the classification of work environments, such as the U.S.
Department of Labor's *Dictionary of Occupational Titles,* particularly the 1939 and 1949 editions. In such approaches, the
basic concept is the job. A job is usually defined as a group of
similar positions in the employing organization. A position is a set
of tasks performed by one person. An occupation is a group of
similar jobs found in several employing organizations. It is clear
from these definitions that the focus is on tasks to be performed.
These tasks are seen as necessary to the attainment of the employer's objectives. Most formal descriptions of the work environment are cast in these terms.

There are a number of other ways of describing the work environment which reflect society's way of evaluating occupations.
In earlier societies occupations were ordered into hierarchies re-
flecting dimensions such as: power (of nobility over slave), religious

status (caste systems), and social philosophy (Spartan versus Athenian ideals). In modern societies occupations are accorded status or prestige for various reasons. Hierarchical ordering of occupations may be based on such diverse considerations as relative importance to the survival of society, degree of intelligence required (Sorokin, 1927); degree of power over others, length of training or education required, monetary compensation, working conditions, and accidents of birth (Osgood & Stagner, 1941). The persistence of occupational prestige hierarchies over time has been noted by such writers as Sorokin (1927) and demonstrated by research findings such as those of Counts (1925) and Deeg and Paterson (1947).

The terms used to describe work environments will also reflect the differing emphases of the various academic disciplines engaged in the study of work. For example industrial engineers would be interested in such matters as work flow, production systems, and time and motion factors; sociologists would study the significance of such aspects of the work environment as group norms, cooperation, authority, communication, and status; economists would focus primarily on labor market problems; physicians would be most interested in aspects of the work environment that affect health. In the same way psychologists would describe the work environment in the terms relevant to their main focus of interest, namely behavior.

One psychological approach to describing the work environment entails its description in terms of worker traits. Such description is based on three premises: workers select work environments congenial to their work personalities; work environments "select" workers with adequate work personalities; it is possible to distinguish among work personalities typically found in different work environments.

Since the pioneering work of Münsterberg (1913) measures of abilities have been used extensively to describe job or occupational requirements. Modern personnel selection methods are based on the establishment of such ability requirements. The most sophisticated use of ability measures in the description of job requirements is exemplified by the work of Paterson and his students (Paterson, Gerken, & Hahn, 1953; Dvorak, 1935, 1947, 1956). This work resulted in the development of *occupational ability patterns*. An occupational ability pattern specifies the minimum level for each of several abilities required in a worker for the prediction of his satisfactory performance in an occupation.

These ability patterns actually describe the work environment in work-personality terms. This description, however, is limited in the sense that it does not attend to the other major set of variables in the work personality, in other words, needs.

Vocational psychologists have long recognized that work provides a major means for satisfying more than just the most basic human needs (food, clothing, shelter). Work has also been studied and discussed in relation to the satisfaction of psychological needs (achievement, authority, independence, creativity). Roe (1956) has called attention to the satisfaction of various human needs in the work setting. Schaffer (1953) has studied the relationship of need satisfaction in work to job satisfaction. Super (1962) is studying the role of work values (needs) in vocational development.

Some attention to the role of need satisfaction in job performance is implicit in the inclusion of both temperament characteristics and interest dimensions (in addition to ability requirements) in the *Worker Trait Requirement for 4,000 Jobs* (1956) of the U.S. Department of Labor. The current edition of the *Dictionary of Occupational Titles* (1965) incorporates this attention to need satisfaction in work by its inclusion of ratings of jobs in terms of the different degrees to which they deal with data, people, and things. This is based on the belief that different temperament and interest factors, in other words, different need patterns, are required for successful performance in different jobs.

An approach to describing the need-satisfying characteristics of the work environment in terms similar to occupational ability patterns is being developed at the University of Minnesota (Weiss et al., 1965). These descriptions are called *occupational reinforcer patterns*. An occupational reinforcer pattern specifies the minimum level for each of several needs required in a worker for the prediction of his satisfaction in a work environment. These reinforcer patterns describe the work environment in work-personality terms but, as in the case of occupational ability patterns, describe only one major set of work-personality variables (needs). A description of the work environment that utilizes both abilities and needs would be useful in conceptualizing how the work personality relates to the world of work.

References

Counts, G. S. The social status of occupations: a problem in vocational guidance. *School Review,* 1925, *33,* 16–27.

Deeg, M. E., & Paterson, D. G. Changes in social status of occupations. *Occupations,* 1947, *25,* 205–208.

Dvorak, B. J. The general aptitude test battery. *Personnel and Guidance Journal,* 1956, *35,* 145–154.

Münsterberg, H., *Psychology and industrial efficiency.* Boston: Houghton, 1913.

Osgood, C. E., & Stagner, R. Analysis of a prestige frame of reference by a gradient technique. *Journal of Applied Psychology,* 1941, *25,* 275–290.

Paterson, D. G., Gerken, C. d'A., & Hahn, M. E. *Revised Minnesota occupational rating scales.* Minneapolis: University of Minnesota Press, 1953.

Roe, A. *The psychology of occupations.* New York: Wiley, 1956.

Schaffer, R. H. Job satisfaction as related to need satisfaction in work. *Psychological Monographs,* 1953, No. 364.

Sorokin, P. *Social mobility.* New York: Harper, 1927.

Super, D. E. The structure of work values in relation to status, achievement, interests, and adjustment. *Journal of Applied Psychology,* 1962, *42,* 231–239.

Weiss, D. J., Dawis, R. V., England, G. W., & Lofquist, L. H. An inferential approach to occupational reinforcement. *Minnesota Studies in Vocational Rehabilitation,* XIX, 1965.

U.S. Department of Labor, Bureau of Employment Security. *Dictionary of occupational titles.* Washington: U.S. Government Printing Office, 1939, 1949, 1965.

U.S. Department of Labor, Bureau of Employment Security. *Worker trait requirements for 4,000 jobs.* Washington: U.S. Government Printing Office, 1956.

5

A Theory of
Work Adjustment

ONE OF THE MAJOR CONCERNS OF VOCATIONAL PSYCHOLOGY, which has long been the object of much research activity, is the description, prediction, and facilitation of work adjustment. In the understanding of work adjustment lies the key to many of the questions raised in the earlier discussion (Chapter 2) of the problems posed by work. While a considerable amount of research has been done, a conceptual framework is needed to organize the accumulated research results, and to give direction to future research activity. In this Chapter, a theory of work adjustment will be proposed to fill this need.

The first formulation of the Theory of Work Adjustment was published in January 1964 as Monograph XV of the *Minnesota Studies in Vocational Rehabilitation*. This theory has provided the conceptual framework for the continuing research program of the Work Adjustment Project in the Industrial Relations Center at the University of Minnesota. Since initial publication of the theory in 1964 considerable progress has been made in developing instruments for measuring variables in the theory and in testing its propositions. With the acquisition of additional research knowledge, and after discussion of the suggestions and criticisms of colleagues, a revision of the theory was published in April, 1968. The following is the 1968 statement of the theory.

The Assumptions of the Theory

The following Theory of Work Adjustment is based on the concept of *correspondence between individual and environment*. Correspondence between an individual and his environment implies conditions that can be described as a harmonious relationship between individual and environment, suitability of the individual to the environment and of the environment for the individual, consonance or agreement between individual and environment, and a reciprocal and complementary relationship between the individual and his environment. Correspondence, then, is a relationship in which the individual and the environment are corresponsive (mutually responsive). Into this relationship the individual brings his requirements of the environment; the environment likewise has its requirements of the individual. In order to survive in an environment the individual must achieve some degree of correspondence.

It is a basic assumption of the Theory of Work Adjustment that *each individual seeks to achieve and maintain correspondence with his environment*. Achieving and maintaining correspondence with the environment are basic motives of human behavior.

There are several kinds of environments—home, school, work —to which an individual must relate. Achieving and maintaining correspondence with one environment may affect the correspondence achieved and maintained in other environments. *Work represents a major environment to which most individuals must relate*.

The individual brings certain skills to the work environment. The work environment provides certain rewards—wages, prestige, personal relationships—to the individual. The individual's skills enable him to respond to the requirements of the work environment. The rewards of the work environment enable it to "respond" to the requirements of the individual. When their minimal requirements are mutually fulfilled, the individual and the work environment are described as correspondent. In the case of work, then, *correspondence can be described in terms of the individual fulfilling the requirements of the work environment, and the work environment fulfilling the requirements of the individual*.

When an individual enters a work environment for the first time, his behavior is directed towards fulfilling its requirements. He also experiences the rewards of the work environment. If he finds a correspondent relationship between himself and the environment, he seeks to maintain it. If he does not, he seeks to establish correspondence or, failing in this, to leave the work environment. There are many different kinds of work environments and many different kinds of individuals, and each work environment-individual relationship is idiosyncratic. In many cases, the initial relationship is not correspondent. In addition, both individuals and work environments are constantly changing. *The continuous and dynamic process by which the individual seeks to achieve and maintain correspondence with his work environment is called work adjustment.*

The achievement of minimal correspondence enables an individual to remain in a work environment. Remaining in the work environment, in turn, allows the individual to achieve more optimal correspondence and to stabilize the correspondent relationship. *This stability of the correspondence between the individual and the work environment is manifested as tenure in the job.*

As correspondence increases, the probability of tenure increases and the projected length of tenure increases as well. Conversely, as correspondence decreases, both the probability of remaining on the job and the projected length of tenure decrease. Tenure is the most basic indicator of correspondence. It can be said, therefore, that *tenure is a function of correspondence between the individual and his work environment.*

From the basic concepts of correspondence and tenure it is possible to develop the concepts of *satisfactoriness* and *satisfaction*. If the individual has substantial tenure, it can be inferred that he has been fulfilling the requirements of the work environment and that the work environment has been fulfilling his requirements. If the individual fulfills the requirements of the work environment, he is defined as a satisfactory worker. If the work environment fulfills the requirements of the individual, he is defined as a satisfied worker. *Satisfactoriness and satisfaction indicate the correspondence between the individual and his work environment.* Satisfactoriness and satisfaction, then, are basic indicators of the degree of success an individual has achieved in maintaining correspondence between himself and his work environment. Satisfactoriness is an *external* indicator of correspondence; it is derived or obtained from sources other than the individual worker's own appraisal of his fulfillment of the requirements of the work environment. Satisfaction is an *internal* indicator of correspondence; it represents the individual worker's appraisal of the extent to which the work environment fulfills his requirements.

With the additional concepts of satisfactoriness and satisfaction it is possible to establish a methodology for predicting tenure.

Satisfactoriness and satisfaction can fluctuate with changes over time in both the individual and the work environment. There are, however, minimum requirements of both the individual and the work environment: minimum levels of satisfactoriness required of the individual and of satisfaction required by the individual. These minimum levels are best established by observing many individuals who have remained in a work environment. *The levels of satisfactoriness and satisfaction observed for a group of individuals with substantial tenure in a specific work environment establish the limits of satisfactoriness and satisfaction from which tenure can be predicted for other individuals.* This is illustrated in Figure 1.

Satisfactoriness and satisfaction can be also viewed as outcomes in the work adjustment process at various points in time during an individual's period of employment. In this sense, they are measures of work adjustment. As measures of work adjustment, satisfactoriness and satisfaction can be used to establish a methodology for the prediction of work adjustment from the assessment of work personalities in relation to work environments. *The work personalities of individuals who fall within the limits of satisfactoriness and satisfaction for which substantial tenure can be predicted may be inferred to be correspondent with the specific work environment.* The different kinds of work personalities for which correspondence is inferred will establish the limits for specific work personality traits necessary for adequate adjustment to the specific work environment. This is illustrated in Figure 2. These limits (for specific personality traits) can be used as a basis for estimating the degree of correspondence between other individuals and each specific work environment. *Work personality–work environment correspondence,* which is estimated in this fashion, *can be used to predict satisfactoriness and satisfaction.*

Figure 1. The Prediction of Tenure

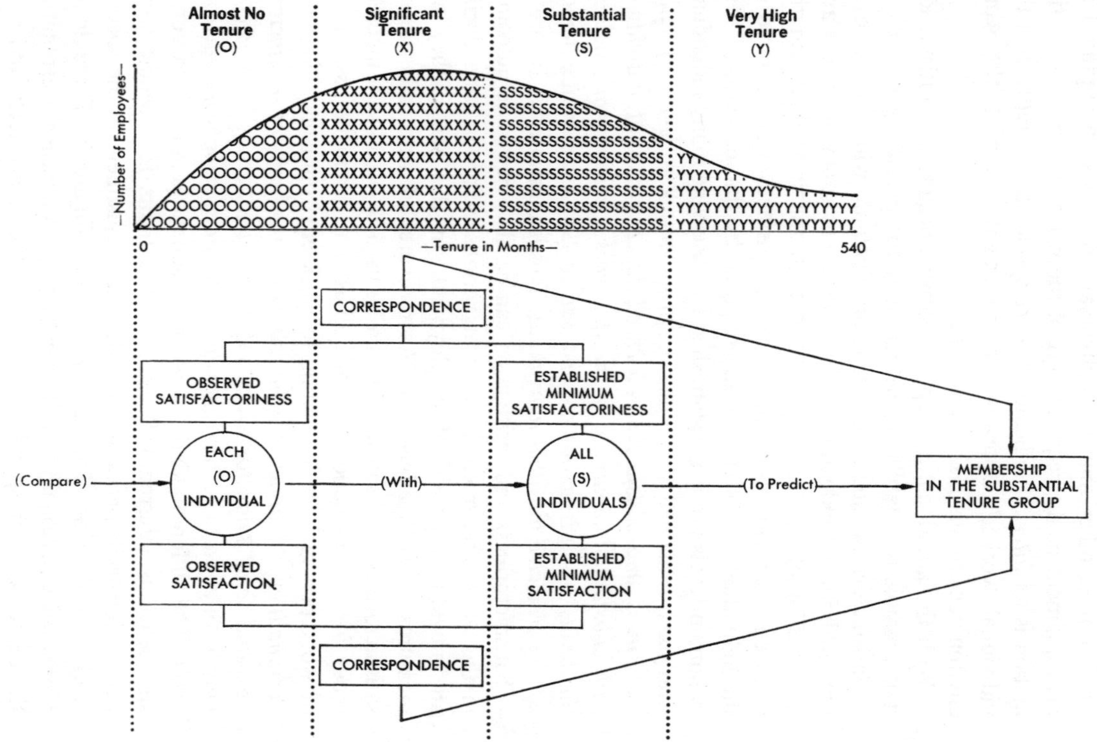

Figure 2. Establishing the Requirements for Work Adjustment

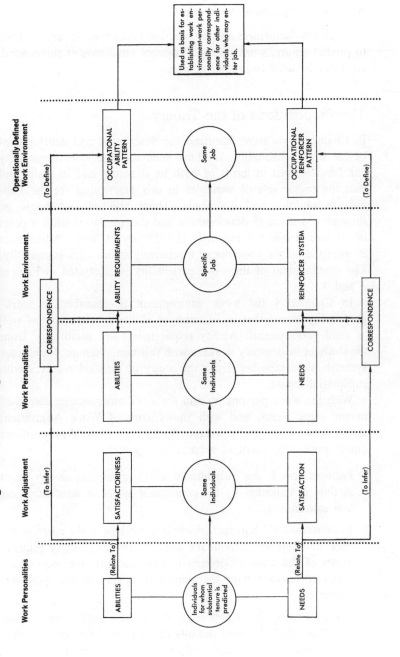

Since satisfactoriness and satisfaction taken together can be used to predict tenure, *work personality—work environment correspondence can be used to predict tenure.*

The Propositions of the Theory

In Chapter 3 we have discussed the description and development of the work personality. We have seen that the work personality can be described in terms of both its structure and its style, and that the major sets of variables in this description are the individual's abilities and his needs. These abilities and needs go through a process of development and differentiation until a point of relative stability is reached. The Theory of Work Adjustment is premised on the existence of a relatively stable work personality. The development of the work personality is illustrated in Figures 3 and 4.

In Chapter 4 the work environment is described in work-personality terms, that is, in terms of ability requirements as well as reinforcer systems. Ability requirements are established from the study of satisfactory workers with substantial tenure. Reinforcer systems are established from the study of satisfied workers with substantial tenure.

With the work personality and the work environment described in the same terms, and with the Theory of Work Adjustment stated above, it is possible to state the following formal propositions about work adjustment as a basis for research:

PROPOSITION I. An individual's work adjustment at any point in time is indicated by his concurrent levels of satisfactoriness and satisfaction.

PROPOSITION II. Satisfactoriness is a function of the correspondence between an individual's abilities and the ability requirements of the work environment, provided that the individual's needs correspond with the reinforcer system of the work environment.

> COROLLARY IIa. Knowledge of an individual's abilities and of his satisfactoriness permits the determination of the effective ability requirements of the work environment.

Figure 3. Inception of the Work Personality

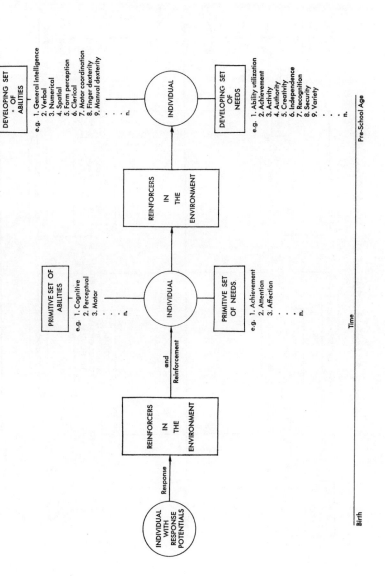

Figure 4. Individuation of the Work Personality

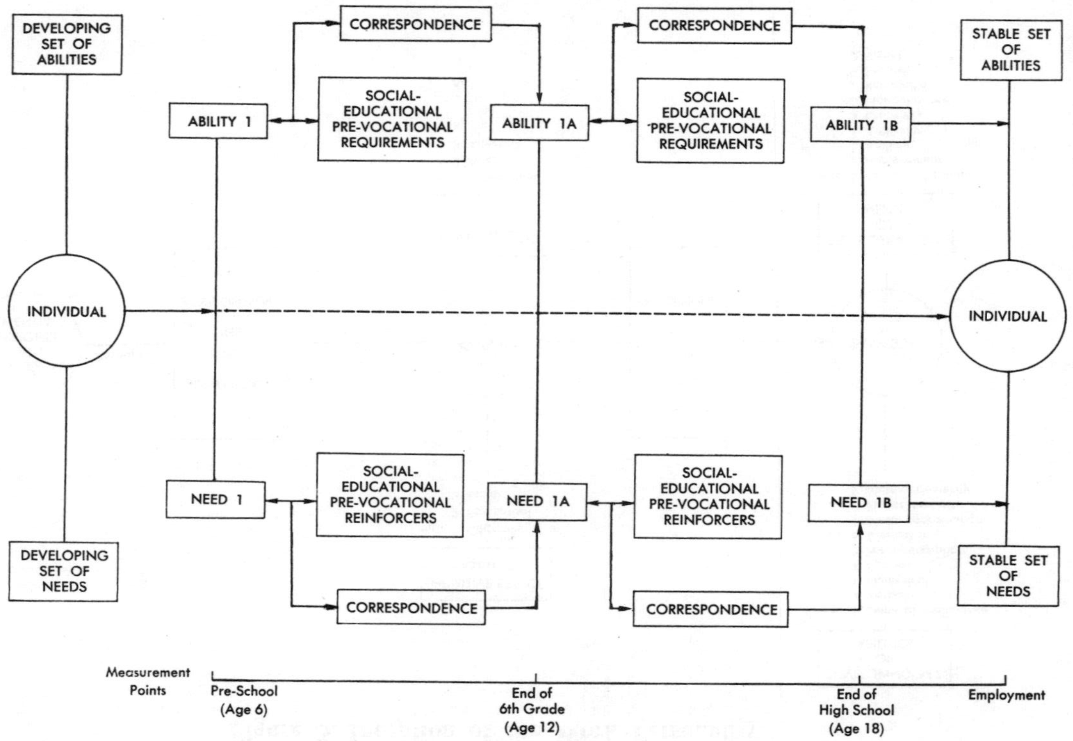

COROLLARY IIb. Knowledge of the ability requirements of the work environment and of an individual's satisfactoriness permits the inference of an individual's abilities.

PROPOSITION III. Satisfaction is a function of the correspondence between the reinforcer system of the work environment and the individual's needs, provided that the individual's abilities correspond with the ability requirements of the work environment.

COROLLARY IIIa. Knowledge of an individual's needs and of his satisfaction permits the determination of the effective reinforcer system of the work environment for the individual.

COROLLARY IIIb. Knowledge of the reinforcer system of the work environment and of an individual's satisfaction permits the inference of an individual's needs.

PROPOSITION IV. Satisfaction moderates the functional relationship between satisfactoriness and ability-requirement correspondence.

PROPOSITION V. Satisfactoriness moderates the functional relationship between satisfaction and need-reinforcer correspondence.

PROPOSITION VI. The probability that an individual will be forced out of the work environment is inversely related to his satisfactoriness.

PROPOSITION VII. The probability that an individual will voluntarily leave the work environment is inversely related to his satisfaction.

Combining Propositions VI and VII, we have:

PROPOSITION VIII. Tenure is a joint function of satisfactoriness and satisfaction.

Given Propositions II, III, and VIII, this corollary follows:

COROLLARY VIIIa. Tenure is a function of ability-requirement and need-reinforcer correspondence.

PROPOSITION IX. Work personality–work environment correspondence increases as a function of tenure.

Figure 5. Work Adjustment

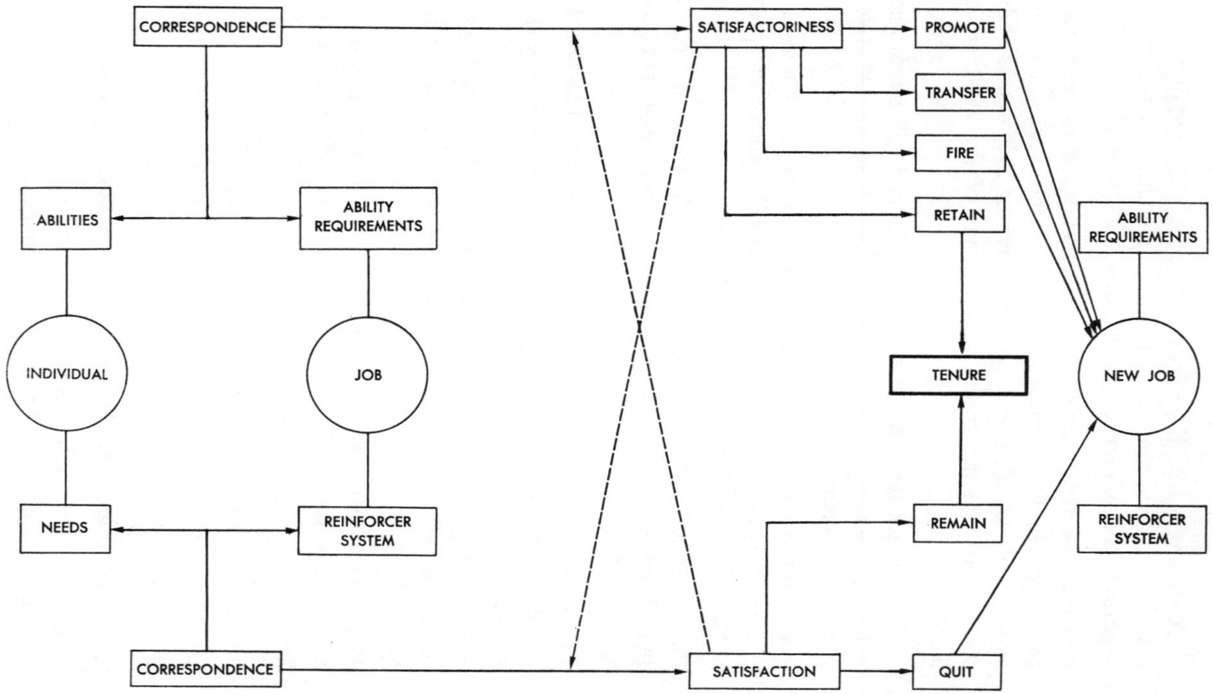

This set of propositions suggests research hypotheses that may be tested to determine the usefulness of the theory in understanding work adjustment. Several of these hypotheses are discussed in Chapter 6. Research evidence in support of the theory is also presented. The schematic model of the theory presented in Figure 5 should assist the reader in visualizing its propositions.

It should be emphasized at this point that the present set of propositions is premised on existing knowledge about work personalities and work environments. This knowledge is, in turn, limited by the current methods used to describe work personalities and work environments. It is felt that work adjustment is very complex and that the present set of propositions may not adequately represent it. Additional research findings and improved methods may suggest other propositions. However, it is felt that a start must be made even with the limited technology available to us at this time.

References

Dawis, R. V., England, G. W., & Lofquist, L. H. A theory of work adjustment. *Minnesota Studies in Vocational Rehabilitation,* XV, 1964.

Dawis, R. V., Lofquist, L. H., & Weiss, D. J. A theory of work adjustment (a revision). *Minnesota Studies in Vocational Rehabilitation,* XXIII, 1968.

6

Research on
Work Adjustment

THERE ARE DATA AVAILABLE FROM SEVERAL EARLY RESEARCH studies which lend credence to the propositions of the Theory of Work Adjustment. Some of these data are found in the research literature dealing with selection and placement problems. Other data have resulted from the continuing research of the Work Adjustment Project at the University of Minnesota. It is, of course, obvious that much additional research must be carried out to test, modify, and develop the theory. This chapter is presented for the reader who is interested in examining the research evidence which tends to support the theory. Suggestions for additional needed research will also be presented.

Research Findings from Early Studies

Viteles' (1924, 1932) development of the job psychograph was one of the earliest attempts to describe the work environment in work-personality terms. This accomplishment suggested the feasibility of a correspondence approach to matching men and jobs, as proposed earlier by Parsons (1909). Viteles' work, however, was limited to the description of ability requirements, and did not attempt to deal with reinforcer systems.

Under the leadership of Professor D. G. Paterson, the Employment Stabilization Research Institute (1935) developed the concept of differential ability patterns in jobs to facilitate the differential selection and placement of individuals. Dvorak (1958) extended this work in the U.S. Department of Labor by her development of a multifactor test battery to describe individuals in terms of job-relevant aptitudes and by her description of work environments in terms of *occupational aptitude patterns* (OAP's).

Past and current research in personnel selection using psychological tests results in the description of jobs in work-personality terms, that is, in terms of minimal ability requirements associated with satisfactory job performance. The literature on the success of this approach is extensive. Examples of this literature may be found in Dunnette (1966), Guion (1965), and Ghiselli (1967).

The publication of aids in vocational counseling and job placement such as the *Minnesota Occupational Rating Scales* (MORS) (Paterson et al., 1941, 1953) and the *Worker Trait Requirements for 4,000 Jobs* (WTR) (1956) illustrates the application of a correspondence approach similar to that proposed by the theory. The MORS was based on ratings of experts and described 432 occupations in terms of seven abilities. The WTR was based on ratings of occupational analysts but included empirically derived OAP's for a limited number of jobs. It also extended the coverage of occupations and included data relevant to reinforcer systems (data on interests, temperaments, and working conditions).

The research of Strong (1943, 1955), Clark (1961), Kuder (1956, 1958), and Campbell (1966) in the area of vocational interest measurement, the research of Super (1962) on work values, and the research of Roe (1956) on needs and their satisfaction in work, are examples of activity relevant to the description of individuals in need terms and the description of work environments in reinforcer-system terms.

The problem of measuring satisfactoriness and satisfaction at work has been the object of numerous research studies. The feasibility of and problems in such measurement have been demonstrated by such studies as those by Rothe (1946a, 1946b; 1947, 1951), Heron (1952), Hardin (1951), and Severin (1952) on satisfactoriness, and by Hoppock (1935), Brayfield and Rothe (1951), and Locke et al. (1964) on satisfaction. An extensive survey of this literature may be found in Scott et al. (1960).

Research relating tenure on the job to satisfactoriness and satisfaction is illustrated in the work of Kerr (1948).

Work Adjustment Project Research

The research being carried out by the staff of the Work Adjustment Project is specifically oriented to the Theory of Work Adjustment. To enable testing of the theory it was necessary to develop instruments to measure the major concepts involved: satisfaction, satisfactoriness, needs, abilities, reinforcer systems, and ability requirements.

An instrument (the Minnesota Satisfaction Questionnaire) has been developed to reliably measure satisfaction with a number of reinforcer classes (with each reinforcer class being measured by a separate scale). The initial studies on the measurement of satisfaction are described in Carlson et al. (1962); the development of the Minnesota Satisfaction Questionnaire is detailed in Weiss et al. (1964a). A manual for the use of the Minnesota Satisfaction Questionnaire has been prepared (Weiss et al., 1967).

The development of an instrument (the Minnesota Satisfactoriness Scales) to measure employment satisfactoriness is reported in Carlson et al. (1963) and Weiss et al. (1966). It was demonstrated that satisfactoriness can be measured independently of satisfaction.

The measurement of work-relevant needs, as defined in the Theory of Work Adjustment, is reported in Weiss et al. (1964a, 1964b). Research to date indicates that a recently developed instrument (the Minnesota Importance Questionnaire) measures these needs independently of satisfaction. Evidence of construct validity was found for several of the scales in the questionnaire.

In the ability measurement area, instruments measuring rather specific work skills have been available to psychologists for several years. For example, a test of typing skill is used to predict typing proficiency on the job, or an eye-hand coordination test is used to predict performance in the assembly of small parts. The Theory of Work Adjustment requires instruments that measure an individual's abilities rather than his specific skills. Abilities are seen as the more basic dimensions underlying work skills. It is therefore necessary to have instruments that sample abilities broadly and that make use of a common normative base, so that relative differences in ability strengths are observable. Multifactor tests seem to meet these requirements best. The General Aptitude Test Battery (1952, 1958) which was developed and standardized on a working population appears to be the most suitable multifactor instrument available to us at this time. Since measures of additional ability dimensions are desirable, work is needed to develop a number of measures to complement those already available.

The measurement of the work environment in terms of ability requirements and reinforcer systems is a major area of current research for the Work Adjustment Project. The development of *occupation ability patterns* (OAP's) and of *occupational reinforcer patterns* (ORP's) for a representative sample of jobs is the goal. Ideally, this sample should represent fields and levels of work (see Roe, 1956) and should be large enough to allow for the possible identification of common ability-requirement and/or reinforcer patterns across levels and fields.

The instruments now available for testing and applying the theory include the following:

The Minnesota Satisfaction Questionnaire (MSQ), to measure the satisfaction of individuals' needs through work (Weiss, Dawis, England, and Lofquist, 1967);

The Minnesota Satisfactoriness Scales (MSS), to measure how satisfactorily individuals perform on their jobs (Weiss, Dawis, Lofquist, and England, 1966);

The Minnesota Importance Questionnaire (MIQ), to measure individuals' vocational needs (Weiss, Dawis, England, and Lofquist, 1964; Weiss, Dawis, Lofquist, and England, 1966);

The Minnesota Job Description Questionnaire (MJDQ), to measure the kinds of reinforcers available in specific jobs and the levels at which they exist (Borgen, Weiss, Tinsley, Dawis, and Lofquist, 1968). Using the MJDQ, Occupational Reinforcer Patterns (ORP's) have been developed for a substantial number of jobs; and

The General Aptitude Test Battery (GATB) (U.S. Department of Labor, 1962b) and its available Occupational Aptitude Pat-

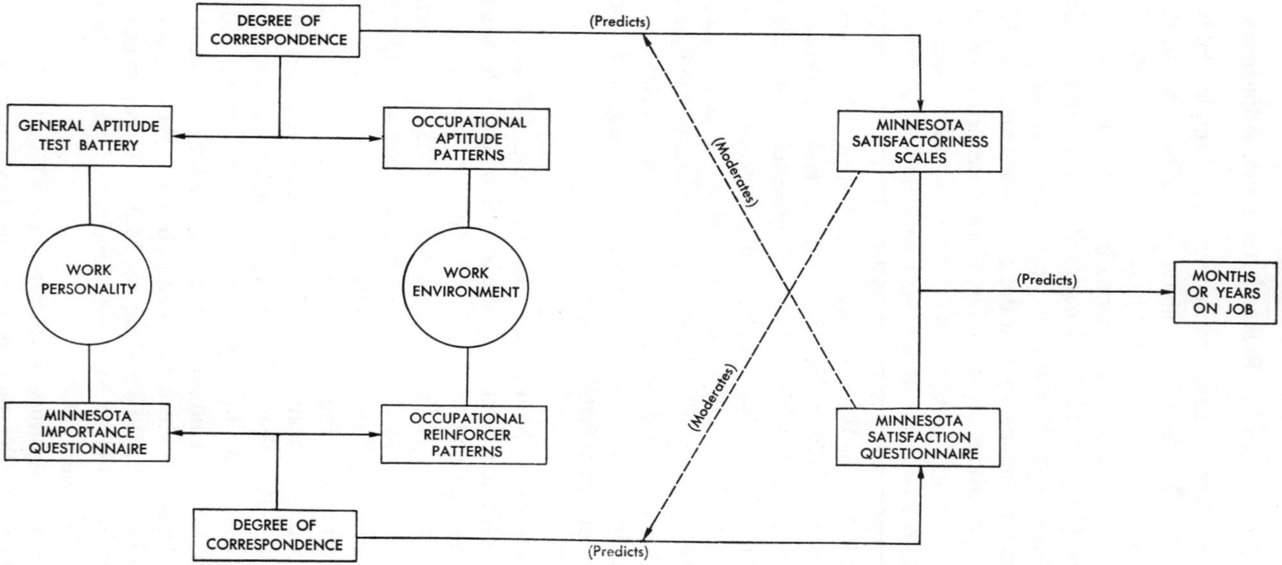

Figure 6. The Theory of Work Adjustment in Operational Terms

terns (OAP's) (U.S. Department of Labor, 1962a) to measure individuals' abilities and to describe the ability requirements of jobs.

The use of these available instruments to operationalize the Theory of Work Adjustment is illustrated in Figure 6.

Sample pages from the instruments that have been developed in the Work Adjustment Project are included in the Appendix to illustrate content and format.

The need for the development of additional psychometrically adequate instruments has limited the research that could be undertaken to test the propositions of the Theory of Work Adjustment (see Chapter 5). It has been possible, however, to conduct some research of this kind. The following research findings lend support to the theory:

1. Measures of satisfactoriness and measures of satisfaction were found to be independent. Table 1 shows the correlations between sets of satisfactoriness and satisfaction scores for six occupational

Table 1

Correlation between Satisfactoriness and Satisfaction

Occupational group	Number in group	Maximum canonical correlation coefficient
Janitors and maintenance men	209	.13
Assemblers	68	.31
Machinists	199	.24
Office clerks	186	.17
Salesmen	165	.11
Engineers	317	.20
Total group	1,144	.12

From: Weiss et al., 1966.

groups. These correlations indicate that the variance common to satisfactoriness and satisfaction is no more than 10 percent for any of the occupational groups. Similar results are reported in Carlson et al. (1963). These findings support the requirement applied in Proposition I that satisfactoriness and satisfaction are independent indicators of work adjustment.

2. When satisfactoriness is predicted from ability test scores, as in the typical selection situation, the closeness of the predicted satisfactoriness to the observed satisfactoriness is a measure of the correspondence between the individual's abilities and the ability requirements of the work environment. This relationship of closeness may be expressed technically by a correlation coefficient. Table 2 shows the correlation coefficients obtained for four occu-

Table 2

Correlation between Predicted and Observed Satisfactoriness

Occupational group	Development		Cross-validation	
	Number in group	Coefficient of correlation	Number in group	Coefficient of correlation
Machinists and assemblers (I)	133	.48	118	.20*
Clerks (I)	93	.35	83	.27*
Clerks (II)	83	.37	93	.18*
Engineers (I)	152	.42	151	.05
Engineers (II)	151	.48	152	.05
Janitors and maintenance men (I)	82	.45	97	.20*
Janitors and maintenance men (II)	97	.33	82	.38**

Note.— This is a double cross-validation study, using reciprocal averages prediction; unpublished data from the Work Adjustment Project. A large group was randomly divided into two groups to enable independent calculation of, and comparison of, correlations for separate groups.
* significant at the .05 level.
** significant at the .01 level.

pational groups. These data lend support to Proposition II which states in part that satisfactoriness is a function of the correspondence between an individual's abilities and the ability requirements of the work environment.

3. Similarly, when satisfaction is predicted from need scores, the closeness of the predicted satisfaction to the observed satisfac-

tion is a measure of the correspondence between the individual's needs and the reinforcer system of the work environment. The data in Table 3 lend support to Proposition III of the theory which states in part that satisfaction is a function of the correspondence between the reinforcer system of the work environment and the individual's needs.

Table 3

Correlation between Predicted and Observed Satisfaction

Group	Development		Cross-validation [a]	
	Number in group	Multiple correlation coefficient	Number in group	Coefficient of correlation
Assemblers, long tenure (I) [b]	99	.59*	98	.38*
Assemblers, long tenure (II) [b]	98	.60*	94	.44*
Assemblers, short tenure	75	.63*	40	.42*
Laborers, short tenure	88	.59	—	—
Laborers, long tenure	77	.63*	40	.22
Managers	90	.56	44	.01
Nurses, full-time (I)	212	.46*	211	.32*
Nurses, full-time (II)	211	.55*	212	.27*
Nurses, part-time (I)	169	.50*	171	.26*
Nurses, part-time (II)	171	.54*	169	.24*
Nurses, supervisory (I)	99	.70**	99	.48**
Nurses, supervisory (II)	99	.68**	99	.30**
Packers, male	68	.64	—	—
Packers, female	34	.92*	—	—
Secretaries	80	.64**	42	.26
Social workers, female	70	.66**	40	−.09

Note.— Unpublished data from the Work Adjustment Project.

[a] correlation obtained on a new sample.

[b] Whenever possible, a large group was randomly divided into two groups to enable independent calculation of, and comparison of, correlations for separate groups.

* significant at the .05 level.

** significant at the .01 level.

4. The prediction of satisfactoriness from ability test scores (see 2. above) was found to be more accurate for groups of individuals with high satisfaction scores than for groups of individuals with low satisfaction scores. Table 4 presents these data. This finding lends support to Proposition IV in the theory which states that satisfaction moderates the functional relationship between satisfactoriness and the correspondence of the individual's abilities with the ability requirements of the work environment.

Studies are under way to test Propositions V–IX.

Table 4

Correlation between Abilities and Satisfactoriness

| | | Satisfactoriness measure | |
Group	Number in group	Productivity	Supervisor evaluation
Total male group	169	.43*	.44*
Male subgroups			
High satisfaction	56	.63*	.69*
Middle satisfaction	57	.48	.52
Low satisfaction	56	.42	.34
Total female group	183	.26*	.27*
Female subgroups			
High satisfaction	61	.63*	.34
Middle satisfaction	61	.29	.33
Low satisfaction	61	.42	.38

Note.— Unpublished data from the Work Adjustment Project.
* significant at .05 level.

Research Needs

In addition to testing the general validity of the propositions of the theory, research should be done on a number of more specific hypotheses which stem from the theory. The following are examples of these hypotheses:

1. Average tenure should be higher for a correspondent group

of individuals (correspondent in both ability-requirement and need-reinforcer terms) than for a non-correspondent group.

2. The proportion of individuals fired for lack of satisfactoriness should be higher for a non-correspondent group (in terms of abilities and requirements) than for a correspondent group.

3. The proportion of individuals who quit voluntarily should be higher for a non-correspondent group (in terms of needs and reinforcers) than for a correspondent group.

4. Low satisfaction would be predicted for a group of individuals whose ability-requirement correspondence is high, but who have left the job after short tenure, or have remained on the job but are judged to lack satisfactoriness.

5. Low satisfactoriness would be predicted for a group of individuals whose need-reinforcer correspondence is high, but who have left the job after short tenure, or have remained on the job but have expressed lack of satisfaction.

6. Work adjustment is also a function of *personality style*. This research hypothesis can be seen as relating to Proposition IX. This proposition states that "work personality–work environment correspondence increases as a function of tenure." Increases in correspondence can occur through changes in the individual, in the environment, or in both the individual and the environment. It is reasonable to assume that the nature of the changes that may take place will be determined to a significant extent by the personality style of the individual who is adjusting to work. Since relatively little research has been done on the relationship of personality style to work adjustment, some attention will be given here to a tentative conceptualization for research that might be productive in this area.

There are basically two ways in which an individual interacts with his work environment. An individual may *act on* his work environment to change it so that it will be more correspondent to his work personality, or an individual may *react to* his work environment by changing the manner in which he expresses his work personality, so that it will be more correspondent to his work environment. These two ways by which an individual may increase correspondence with his work environment may be termed *modes of work adjustment*. The first way might be called the *active mode,* the second the *reactive mode.* With respect to their typical mode of adjustment, individuals may be described as *active* or *reactive.*

An individual's typical mode of adjustment can be predicted from his response and reinforcement history. In a specific work situation, however, an individual's mode of adjustment is likely to be affected by the flexibility or rigidity of the work environment, that is, of its requirement and reinforcer characteristics. If the work environment is flexible, the active individual can change it to increase correspondence. If the work environment is rigid, the active individual cannot change it and will find it necessary to leave the environment or to try to adopt a reactive mode of adjusting. In contrast, the reactive individual is relatively unaffected by the flexibility or rigidity of his work environment.

Since the work environment may be described in terms of such characteristics as flexibility or rigidity, it may be thought of as having a "style" much in the same way as we think of an individual's personality style. The "structure" of the work environment, on the other hand, would include its ability requirements and its reinforcer system.

It should be possible to describe the work personalities of individuals who use active or reactive modes of adjustment. One immediate research need would be the identification of the significant dimensions of personality style. For example, an individual's *flexibility* or *rigidity* might be one of these dimensions, and it might be approached by studying the precision of correspondence required by an individual for his satisfaction.

In addition, one might expect individuals who use active or reactive modes of adjustment to exhibit characteristic patterns of abilities and needs in their personality structures. This suggests research hypotheses such as the following examples:

An individual who typically uses the *active* mode of adjustment would exhibit (1) extremely high levels of one or a few abilities, in combination with high levels of such needs as ability utilization, achievement, and closure (needs requiring intrinsic satisfaction), or (2) dominance of motor or effector abilities in the total ability pattern, in combination with preferences (needs) for reinforcers that will give intrinsic instead of extrinsic satisfaction.

An individual whose typical mode of adjustment is *reactive* would exhibit (1) relatively high levels for several abilities, but lower overall intra-individual variability for his total ability pattern than the active individual (his preferences for reinforcers will be for those yielding extrinsic satisfaction), or (2) dominance of receptor or sensory-input abilities in the total ability pattern, in combination with needs requiring extrinsic satisfaction.

It should also be possible to identify individuals who will use active or reactive modes of adjustment from both life-history data and psychometric data. The relevance of life-history data to modes of adjustment is supported by such studies as that by Warnken and Siess (1965). Instruments such as the Strong Vocational Interest Blank, the Minnesota Vocational Interest Inventory, and the Minnesota Multiphasic Personality Inventory would seem to provide the item contents that would be useful for psychometric identification.

It is obvious that more research is needed to substantiate the propositions of the Theory of Work Adjustment and to test the research hypotheses derived from it. Priorities should be given to the refinement of the instruments that are available (for the measurement of satisfaction, satisfactoriness, needs, and abilities) and to the development of methods for describing the work environment in work-personality terms (that is, in terms of ability requirements and reinforcer systems).

The applicability of the theory to the study of special groups, such as the disabled and racial minorities, should be investigated. An example of such an application may be found in the monograph entitled *Disability and Work* (Lofquist et al., 1964). As indicated in this publication, application of the theory to special groups may require modification of currently available measuring instruments and/or the development of new ones.

In order to relate the theory to other areas of special interest in vocational psychology and in order to amplify the concept of the work personality, additional research is needed on how abilities and needs develop in individuals and on how ability development is related to need development. Chapter 3 includes a discussion of the possible genesis of these work-personality variables and their developmental interrelationships. Longitudinal studies will be required to substantiate the authors' conceptualization of these variables in the developing work personality. Research could be addressed to such questions as these:

—Are there any evidences of work-relevant ability and need development in early play activity?
—How is an individual's response and reinforcement history related to the development of abilities and needs?
—At what age do ability and need strengths become stable?
—Do specific ability and need strengths decline with the absence of appropriate response and reinforcement experience?
—Are ability and need patterns for individuals with restricted response and reinforcement histories (such as disadvantaged persons) amenable to change?

Answers to questions such as these not only are important for the development and/or modification of the Theory of Work Adjustment, but also have implications for the understanding and treatment of social problems. The next Chapter discusses some of the social implications of the theory.

References

Borgen, F. H., Weiss, D. J., Tinsley, H. E. A., Dawis, R. V., & Lofquist, L. H. Occupational Reinforcer Patterns. *Minnesota Studies in Vocational Rehabilitation,* XXIV, 1968.

Brayfield, A. H., & Rothe, H. F. An index of job satisfaction. *Journal of Applied Psychology,* 1951, *35,* 307-311.

Campbell, D. P. *Manual for Strong Vocational Interest Blanks, Revised,* Stanford, California: Stanford University Press, 1966.

Carlson, R. E. A test of selected hypotheses from the Theory of Work Adjustment. Unpublished doctoral dissertation, University of Minnesota, 1965.

Carlson, R. E., Dawis, R. V., England, G. W., & Lofquist, L. H. The measurement of employment satisfaction. *Minnesota Studies in Vocational Rehabilitation,* XIII, 1962.

Carlson, R. E., Dawis, R. V., England, G. W., & Lofquist, L. H.

The measurement of employment satisfactoriness. *Minnesota Studies in Vocational Rehabilitation,* XIV, 1963.

Clark, K. E. *The vocational interests of non-professional men.* Minneapolis: University of Minnesota Press, 1961.

Dawis, R. V., Weiss, D. J., Lofquist, L. H., & Betz, E. Satisfaction as a moderator in the prediction of satisfactoriness. *Proceedings, 75th Annual Convention, American Psychological Association,* 1967, 269-270.

Dunnette, M. D. *Personnel selection and placement.* Belmont, California: Wadsworth, 1966.

Dvorak, B. J. Differential occupational ability patterns. *Bulletin of the Employment Stabilization Research Institute,* Vol. III, No. 3, February 1935.

Dvorak, B. J. The general aptitude test battery. In Super, D. E. (Ed.), *The use of multifactor tests in guidance.* Washington: American Personnel and Guidance Association, 1958.

Ghiselli, E. E. *The validity of occupational aptitude tests.* New York: Wiley, 1966.

Guion, R. M. *Personnel testing.* New York: McGraw, 1965.

Hardin, E. *Measurement of physical output at the job level.* Research and Technical Report 10, Industrial Relations Center, University of Minnesota, 1951.

Heron, A. A. A psychological study of occupational adjustment. *Journal of Applied Psychology,* 1952, *36,* 385-387.

Hoppock, R. *Job satisfaction.* New York: Harper, 1935.

Kerr, W. A. On the validity and reliability of the job satisfaction tear ballot. *Journal of Applied Psychology,* 1948, *32,* 275-281.

Kuder, G. F. *Kuder Preference Record—Vocational.* Chicago: Science Research Associates, 1956.

Kuder, G. F. *Kuder Preference Record—Occupational.* Chicago: Science Research Associates, 1958.

Locke, E. A., Smith, P. C., Kendall, L. M., Hulin, C. L., & Miller, A. Convergent and discriminant validity for areas and methods of rating job satisfaction. *Journal of Applied Psychology,* 1964, *48,* 313-319.

Lofquist, L. H., Siess, T. F., Dawis, R. V., England, G. W., & Weiss, D. J. Disability and work. *Minnesota Studies in Vocational Rehabilitation,* XVII, 1964.

Parsons, F. *Choosing a vocation.* Boston: Houghton, 1909.

Paterson, D. G., Gerken, C. d'A., & Hahn, M. E. *The Minnesota occupational rating scales*. Chicago: Science Research Associates, 1941.

Paterson, D. G., Gerken, C. d'A., & Hahn, M. E. *Revised Minnesota occupational rating scales*. Minneapolis: University of Minnesota Press, 1953.

Roe, A. *The psychology of occupations*. New York: Wiley, 1956.

Rothe, H. F. Output rates among butter wrappers. I. Work curves and their stability. *Journal of Applied Psychology*, 1946a, *30*, 199-211.

Rothe, H. F. Output rates among butter wrappers. II. Frequency distributions and an hypothesis regarding the "restriction of output." *Journal of Applied Psychology*, 1946b, *30*, 320-327.

Rothe, H. F. Output rates among machine operators. I. Distributions and their reliability. *Journal of Applied Psychology*, 1947, *31*, 484-489.

Rothe, H. F. Output rates among chocolate dippers. *Journal of Applied Psychology*, 1951, *35*, 94-97.

Scott, T. B., Dawis, R. V., England, G. W., & Lofquist, L. H. A definition of work adjustment. *Minnesota Studies in Vocational Rehabilitation*, X, 1960.

Severin, D. The predictability of various kinds of criteria. *Personnel Psychology*, 1952, *5*, 93-104.

Strong, E. K., Jr. *Vocational interests of men and women*. Stanford University Press, 1943.

Strong, E. K., Jr. *Vocational interests 18 years after college*. Minneapolis: University of Minnesota Press, 1955.

U.S. Department of Labor, Bureau of Employment Security, USES. *Guide to the use of the General Aptitude Test Battery: Section III. Development*. Washington: U.S. Government Printing Office, 1952-1956.

U.S. Department of Labor, Bureau of Employment Security, USES. Technical report on standardization of General Aptitude Test Battery. *Technical Report B-381*, July 1958.

U.S. Department of Labor, U.S. Employment Service. *Worker trait requirements for 4000 jobs*. Washington: U.S. Government Printing Office, 1956.

Viteles, M. S. Vocational guidance and job analysis: the psychological viewpoint. *Psych. Clin.*, *15*, 1924, 164.

Viteles, M. S. *Industrial psychology*. New York: Norton, 1932.

Warnken, R. G., & Siess, T. F. The use of the cumulative record in the prediction of behavior. *Personnel and Guidance Journal,* 1965, *44,* 3, 231–237.

Weiss, D. J., Dawis, R. V., England, G. W., & Lofquist, L. H. Construct validation studies of the Minnesota Importance Questionnaire. *Minnesota Studies in Vocational Rehabilitation,* XVIII, 1964. (a)

Weiss, D. J., Dawis, R. V., England, G. W., & Lofquist, L. H. The measurement of vocational needs. *Minnesota Studies in Vocational Rehabilitation,* XVI, 1964. (b)

Weiss, D. J., Dawis, R. V., England, G. W., & Lofquist, L. H. Manual for the Minnesota Satisfaction Questionnaire. *Minnesota Studies in Vocational Rehabilitation,* XXII, 1967.

Weiss, D. J., Dawis, R. V., Lofquist, L. H., & England, G. W. Instrumentation for the Theory of Work Adjustment. *Minnesota Studies in Vocational Rehabilitation,* XXI, 1966.

7

Implications
of the Theory

MANY OF THE SOCIAL PROBLEMS OF OUR TIMES ARE INTIMATELY bound up with work. This is illustrated in broad problem areas such as unemployment, automation, retirement, disability, and poverty. These are matters of national as well as individual concern. At the level of the individual, the family, and the employer, we find these social problems taking the form of difficulties with vocational choice, selection and placement, employee morale, boredom and monotony, anomie, turnover, changing jobs, retraining, and identifying appropriate extra-work and social activities.

It seems obvious that a developing psychology of work has significant contributions to make towards the solution or alleviation of many of our social problems. The Theory of Work Adjustment, as a part of the developing psychology of work, provides a way of conceptualizing some of these major social problems. Viewing these problems in the context of the theory may suggest new emphases or approaches that are complementary to those now being used. The following brief discussions of some of the broad social problem areas may serve as illustrations.

Unemployment

Current approaches to unemployment as a national problem include acceleration of placement activities in public agencies, identification of shortage occupations, retraining, relocation of workers, and creation of new jobs. All too often these approaches tend to focus on the total group of "the unemployed" with its statistically average worker. That is, approaches to unemployment are geared to the hypothetical individual with one general set of characteristics (average age, abilities, needs, and so forth). With the knowledge of the facts of individual differences, one would expect that such group programs will not be appropriate for large numbers of individuals.

The Theory of Work Adjustment stresses the need for individualized matching of men and jobs. This emphasis suggests that such activities as placement and retraining should be based on a careful analysis both of the individual's unique abilities and needs and of the available work environments. This individualized approach is likely to yield solutions that are more lasting than those achieved through programs for the retraining of unemployed workers for shortage occupations, when these programs are undertaken without proper regard for correspondence between work personalities and work environments. That is, the solutions obtained by the use of an individualized approach might be more satisfactory to employers and more satisfying to individuals, and more effective in terms of improved tenure, in the sense that employees stay in the same position longer or move across positions or jobs in an orderly and progressive fashion. (Movement across several jobs with similar work environments would be viewed as consistent with work adjustment.)

In order to make feasible the individualized approach to the unemployment problem, it is necessary that professional personnel be trained in the assessment of work personalities and work environments, that assessment tools be utilized and further developed, that information on work environments be developed in relevant terms and for many jobs, and that detailed procedures for matching men and jobs be made available.

Some might view such an individualized approach to the problem of unemployment as impractical both because of the magnitude of the task and because of the large expenditure of money required. It is interesting to note, however, that a governmental program dealing with similar reemployment problems, involving large numbers of people, and using an individualized approach was highly successful. We are referring to the prototype program carried out by the Veterans Administration in its rehabilitation of the veterans of World War II (Scott, 1945). It is also interesting to note that a recent development in the retraining activity under the Manpower Development and Training Act is the approval of multi-occupational training programs. This is a step in the direction of individualized retraining opportunities. It should increase the likelihood of appropriate training and appropriate subsequent employment being available to individuals.

The individualized approach to matching men and jobs may have an additional salutary effect in reducing the feelings of clients that they are being treated impersonally by bureaucracy. Stereotypes of "the unemployed" and "jobs for the unemployed" might give way to a focus on the utilization in work of the unique personality characteristics of each individual.

Automation

As increasing numbers of workers are displaced from their jobs by technological advances in industrial techniques and machines, our society is faced with the need to find suitable ways to relocate people in jobs. Many of these technologically displaced workers are older persons who have substantial tenure in their kind of work, little experience in job seeking, little information about the labor market, and, probably, little desire to change.

Society has reacted to the problem of automation in several ways. The strongest reaction is the fear (almost panic) that the steady encroachment of automation on employment opportunities will soon leave us with no jobs, or, at best, with a severely restricted number of jobs. There is, of course, some basis for this fear. It is also, however, reminiscent of the fears expressed during the first industrial revolution.

When a worker is technologically displaced, the first thought seems to be that he must be retrained—and retrained for higher-level work. If this is really a requirement for any worker affected by automation, one would have to assume that all other similar positions across firms were automated and, in addition, all positions in the job family, and across all job families at that level of work and the levels below it were automated. We would suspect that these assumptions are not quite warranted. Perhaps workers do not have to be retrained, as a general rule, and perhaps the relocation need not be sought at a higher level. Perhaps also the reemployment of a technologically displaced person requires a program approach that provides for individualized study of each worker's problem, with particular reference to the nature of his work personality, and to the appropriateness for him of the job that was automated.

The Theory of Work Adjustment provides a context for viewing the traumatic effects of being technologically displaced. A radical change is experienced by the worker. This change is the sudden removal of the job requirement-reinforcer system in which the individual has been operating. His primary problem is one of discovering what other correspondent work environments are available to him after technological change has occurred.

The problem of automation is essentially the problem of moving from one job to another, except that the move is more sudden and may be more traumatic than one initiated by the worker himself. It is forced only from the employer's side, and may occur after an individual's abilities and needs are firmly crystallized. There is nothing that requires the worker's movement from one job to another to be in a vertical direction. If he was adjusted to the position that he must now leave, it would appear more reasonable that his movement be in a horizontal direction, or on a slight plane from horizontal. It would seem sensible to defer any decisions to retrain technologically displaced workers (at any level) until careful assessments of their work personalities have been made and the appropriateness of other work environments for their work adjustment has been explored.

The most promising approaches to the achievement of work adjustment for workers displaced by automation would appear to be those which are concerned with identifying the jobs (at broad skill levels of work, and across levels and fields of work) which have common job requirement–job reinforcer characteristics. In addition, there is an evident need for well-trained vocational counselors to assist individuals in learning both about their own work personalities and about the appropriate—and available—work environments.

Retirement

Modern society with its higher standards of living, its public health controls, and its advances in medical treatment, has succeeded in establishing a higher level of life expectancy for its workers. Yet while increasing numbers of workers live longer and have available to themselves more years of potentially productive work activity, society's accepted ages for required or voluntary retirement have not changed appreciably. Many workers who can and want to continue working must leave their jobs for retirement. They are also in a very real sense expected by society to be happy with the fact that they have achieved the status of retirement, whether or not they share that view. The occasion is usually celebrated with extra reinforcements of a non-recurring type from the work organization: the dinner, the praise, the watch, the pin, the bonus check. Then the retired individual is expected to "settle down" to the one remaining work-environment reinforcer (often one with reinforcement value reduced to almost an imperceptible level), his continuing retirement check. On the other hand, there seem to be a great many individuals who see retirement as their reward for years of hard work, who work for it as an ultimate goal, and who want to retire as soon as the system will permit.

In either case—whether the worker is required to retire, or whether he wishes to retire—it is likely that relatively few individuals have planned a retirement with which they become satisfied. This is because many of them have viewed retirement only in a rather vague or abstract way as an expected state of affairs that should somehow change their lives in desirable directions.

Increased recreational activity is supposed to characterize the retired individual. Now that he has the time, he is expected to golf, camp, boat, dance, play chess, paint, and the like. He is expected to do these things because he is now supposedly "free to do them," whether or not he has ever learned to do or to prefer them. Perhaps the stereotype of what retired executives do, plus a desire at some point in later life to reach equality with others in the occupational hierarchy, have influenced society to think of retirement in terms of recreational and leisure-time activities. The fact that society does think this way is evidenced by the planning that is done to increase park and recreational areas and leisure centers for older persons. It seems to be assumed that when people retire they will not only be able to change but will also *want* to change their life styles; and that they should be encouraged to participate in recreational activities.

Increasing recreational and leisure-time facilities will provide some activity outlets for many people. It should be remembered, however, that nationally popular leisure-time activities are engaged in by only a small part of the total population; that there are individual differences in kinds of activities which are preferred; and that there is probably a large segment of the working population that participates in few, if any, such activities. It may be unwarranted to assume that retirement will greatly increase the number of new participants in recreational activities.

As one worker in his first year of retirement put it, "It ain't easy to recreate." Perhaps many others share his experience. When the high school or college teacher tells his young students that, whether or not they are aware of it, they are already in the last stages of preparing for their retirement, he makes an important point.

All of this suggests that society's problem of retirement is not simply one of the increase in numbers of older persons (and one that will be only partially solved by increases in leisure-time facilities). It is a problem that requires attention to the individualization of retirement, and that might focus less on expected changes in mature people and more on what these people bring to retirement.

The Theory of Work Adjustment provides a context in which the problem of retirement can be viewed somewhat differently. The theory would suggest that the retired individual seeks to function in his new environment in much the same fashion as he has operated in the work environment. He brings a stable work personality (abilities and needs) to retirement, and he finds requirements and reinforcers in the retirement environment. The new environment of requirements and reinforcers is defined by his remaining work-related functions and by his avocational activities. The retired person brings to this new environment certain abilities and certain needs which are well established. He can do certain things, and some things better than others; and he has experienced certain ways in which his needs can best be satisfied. His work-related activities have become, in most cases, severely restricted. His avoca-

tional activities occupy the larger share of his time. These avocational activities must then supply the response opportunities for
utilizing his abilities, and the reinforcement conditions for satisfying his needs.

The community regulates avocational activities in the sense that
it prescribes requirements which must be met if an individual
wishes to continue to participate. Reinforcement for avocational
activity can also be described in terms of avocational reinforcer
systems. It would seem that adjustment to retirement (that is, the
achievement of a retirement that is both satisfactory and satisfying)
can be viewed in the same terms as work adjustment; in other words,
individual abilities and needs should be matched with environmental requirement-reinforcer conditions. Thus, instead of relying
on radical readjustment in individuals (which there appears to be
no good reason to expect) one would focus on continued adjustment in a changed environment for an individual with a stable
personality. Instead of trying to change people one would seek to
help them function within the framework of their established personalities.

In order to explore the implications of the Theory of Work Adjustment in facing retirement problems it will be necessary to
utilize the individual assessment tools available for measuring abilities and needs; to carry out careful analyses of the retirement environments (analogous to thorough job analyses); to describe retirement environments in requirement and reinforcer terms; and to
provide retirement counselors trained to assist individuals in
achieving the "personality-environment correspondences" that will
ensure adjustment.

Disability

The problems of integrating the physically and/or psychiatrically
disabled into the social and economic communities have been
viewed in a variety of ways. At one point in history the impaired
person was viewed socially as an object to be feared and avoided.
His disability was seen in contexts of religious beliefs and super-
stition. Society accepted no responsibility for him. Later, the

prevailing view took the opposite direction and the impaired person was regarded as an object of pity and/or as someone who must be protected and cared for. Medical treatment was provided for impaired persons, but disability continued to be viewed only in the context of the anatomically perfect man. Competence for work and for participation in the normal activities of society was determined solely on the basis of whether or not the individual was anatomically whole.

Today, medicine's modern functional concept of disability rejects the focus on anatomical perfection in determining suitability for employment (Rusk, 1958). Instead, treatment and retraining restore as much capacity as possible, and the individual is encouraged to utilize all his remaining assets fully. World War II, with its emphasis on rehabilitating disabled servicemen, provided the climate in which this change in viewpoint could take place. Society added a strong focus on integration of the disabled into the economic and social structures to the existing focus on protection and care.

Psychologically, disability has come to be viewed in the context of the concept of the person as a whole interacting with the environment (Garrett & Levine, 1962), or in terms of the variations in physique which influence the reactions of others to the disabled individual, or of the disabled individual to himself (Wright, 1960). Viewing disability with the focus on these psychological aspects adds important new dimensions to the understanding and treatment of disabled persons. However, psychological aspects still tend to be studied more often for medically classified groups than for individuals with an impairment. The literature of what might be termed "psychology as applied to disability" recognizes the facts of individual differences in people (including disabled people), but seems to continue to deal mainly with stereotypically labeled groups such as "cardiacs" or "the cerebral palsied." Medically oriented classification systems are in widespread use. Perhaps this is to be expected in view of the traditional position of medicine as the initial and most active group in the treatment and restoration of disabled persons.

As society assumed responsibility for dealing with the problem of disability, it established the concept of rehabilitation and defined this as the "restoration of the handicapped to the fullest physical, mental, social, vocational, and economic usefulness of which they are capable" (National Council on Rehabilitation, 1942). There are, of course, other definitions. Social and vocational usefulness and individual independence are stressed, as one would expect them to be in our society.

To achieve rehabilitation for those individuals with disability, a large federal-state network of rehabilitation agencies has been built up in this country over the last forty-five years. Its goals have included treatment, training, and placement, with the primary focus on the adjustment of disabled individuals to a life of productive employment whenever possible. The active agent in rehabilitation who counsels, places, and coordinates activities with other professional workers, and who evaluates success and innovates special techniques, is the vocational rehabilitation counselor. He has done an excellent job under the aegis of the federal and state agencies. Unfortunately, however, his case load is overwhelming; the number of individuals he rehabilitates grows substantially from year to year, but not fast enough; and he seems to have reached a plateau with regard to his innovations in techniques. Funds are available to expand rehabilitation greatly. Society is, in fact, demanding rapid expansion. Training programs are expanding, but the ratio of trained personnel to position openings for vocational rehabilitation counselors cannot become favorable in the foreseeable future if we adhere to our present ways of working with disabled persons and of training competent counselors.

Perhaps some of the answers to meeting the social problem of disability can be found in a change in focus. Recognizing the necessity of the medical focus in treatment, and the importance of social and psychological factors in understanding the over-all impact of disability, it may still be necessary to approach the problems of vocational rehabilitation with applications derived from a more work-relevant and individualized-treatment standpoint. Medical diagnostic categories are obviously essential for their medical treatment and subsequent regimen implications. After maximal medical treatment, however, we should be concerned with the relevance of changes (imposed by disabling conditions) for the work adjustment of a unique individual.

In the context of the Theory of Work Adjustment, disability

is defined as significant decreases in the abilities of an individual brought about by physical, mental, and/or emotional trauma, with or without accompanying changes in the person's needs. Significant decreases are those for which there are changes in ability-requirement correspondence for current, continuing, or beginning work adjustment. Such changes will have predictable consequences in the correspondences with ability requirements and reinforcer systems in jobs that can be attained by the individual. Disability is viewed, therefore, in terms of its actual disruptive consequences for a unique individual, as these relate to predictions of work adjustment, rather than in terms of the expectations for work success for an individual viewed against the average person in a particular disability class or its stereotype. The theory focuses more specifically and intensively on the work-adjustment potential of an individual than appears to be the case in contemporary thinking and practice in rehabilitation. Lofquist et al. (1964) have described in more detail the treatment of disability and work within the context of the Theory of Work Adjustment.

Let us examine some of the implications for practice which arise when disability is viewed literally as loss of skill that has relevance for correspondence with job-ability requirements (with attention also given to need-reinforcer-system correspondence).

Instead of assigning vocational rehabilitation counselors to disability areas as specialists in an area (a current trend), counselors would work across all disability categories. They would in a very real sense become experts in assessing ability and need dimensions for work, and changes or loss in abilities and needs, rather than functioning as experts in a disability category.

It is quite possible that the assessment of abilities and needs, the matching of work personalities and work environments, and the predictions for work adjustment, could be done by technicians supervised by trained professional vocational rehabilitation counselors. In this event, professional counselors would have more time for the demanding communication and therapeutic aspects of rehabilitation counseling. Such a division of labor, and for that matter application of the theory, will depend to a large extent upon the availability of ability- and need-measuring instruments, the availability of job requirement and reinforcer system information, and the description of procedures for determining necessary correspondences to predict work adjustment. Some of this necessary technology is available at the present time (see Chapter 9).

Poverty

Recent legislation has made the elimination of poverty a major national goal. We are seeking to raise the standard of living of the poor, principally through programs to enrich the environment (housing, education, and recreation programs), to upgrade job skills (training and retraining programs), and to provide greater economic opportunities (job placement, relocation, and fair employment programs). These programs employ teachers, counselors, social workers, and other specialists in efforts to effect changes not only in the environments of socioeconomically disadvantaged people, but also in their basic personalities.

While we would not question the need to work intensely and immediately on the problems of poverty, it would appear that the sudden intensification of the attack on poverty has led us to place an unwarranted faith in our ability to change personalities. We also seem to be assuming that individuals who are classified in the poverty group have uniformly low levels of abilities and a common pattern of psychological needs. These assumptions are not supported by the facts of individual differences.

The Theory of Work Adjustment leads us to expect that most of the physically mature individuals served by anti-poverty programs are also psychologically mature, in other words, that they have crystallized and stable work personalities (abilities and needs). This suggests that the focus of professional services should be on the utilization of each individual's abilities and the satisfaction of his needs, rather than on changing his ability and need structures. This further suggests the need for more emphasis on individualized counseling, training, and placement for work environments consonant with the individual's existing work personality. Such an approach requires careful individual assessment of work personalities and the development of occupational information which will describe work environments in the same terms.

This approach seems more realistic and more likely to produce lasting results because it is based specifically on the prediction of work adjustment.

The Theory of Work Adjustment also has implications for programs for enriching the environments of poverty-area children. These are discussed in the section which follows.

Education

Through its vast educational system society is moving to meet such problems as the effects of deficient educational-social backgrounds, the inefficient use of educational facilities and tools in the face of augmented enrollments, and the growing depersonalization of the student because of increasingly unfavorable teacher-student ratios. Actions taken to meet such problems appear to focus on the size of the problem, the general category into which the problem falls, and the availability of new equipment to carry out more efficiently the techniques in education that have been long established. For example, we observe that facilities are being utilized for longer periods of time during the school year; that "impoverished children" are starting school earlier for a "head start"; that educational television is being utilized to reach larger student groups; that selected groups of students are getting more extensive subject matter in enriched course offerings; that teachers are being exhorted to foster creativity in students; that school counselors are assisting students in making an orderly transition through the school years; and that large numbers of students are being encouraged to go on to college.

Such measures are helpful and necessary in responding to current social pressures, but they do not represent the kind of sophisticated and long-range approach that is needed to meet these problems effectively. Such an approach requires a systematic conceptualization of the goals and problems of modern education. With due respect for the goals of Project Head Start, but to illustrate the need for a conceptual framework, one might ask such questions as: What experiences will best prepare the children for entrance into formal classes? How do the children differ individually with respect to their experiential histories? How can knowledge of their behavior in preschool settings be used to facilitate continued progress in school? What new techniques can be developed for teachers? The answers given to such questions tend to be too general. They include remarks to the effect that "after so much impoverishment they need every stimulation they can get," "the Head Start pupils enjoy themselves," and "certainly the experiences must help them." In other words, the implication is that any kind of program that introduces new experiences for this group is intrinsically good. While this is probably true, it would appear that more effective work with such a group would result from a more definitive conceptualization of both the problems and the goals, and from knowledge of human behavior based on research.

The context of the Theory of Work Adjustment provides one approach to conceptualizing these problems. It suggests that, in educational research, more attention be given to the developing work personality, and particularly to the identification and measurement of ability requirements and reinforcer systems in specific educational and social environments. In order effectively to develop, in individuals, the abilities and needs compatible with the realities of work environments, educators must know how to structure and sequence educational experiences for optimal ability utilization and need satisfaction.

With adequate information on the ability requirements and reinforcer systems of educational and social environments, and with data on the abilities and needs of students, the educator might find it possible to determine in more detail how school experiences influence the development of their work personalities, and what range of experiences is necessary to allow for the development and stabilization of their abilities and needs. With education conceptualized in this fashion, society might come to a proper appreciation of the range of individual differences in the work personalities of students. It might then become more socially acceptable for academically "bright" students to go into "vocational" work (trades or jobs below the professional level). We might even be able to speak seriously of courses such as "enriched woodworking."

References

Garrett, J. F., & Levine, E. S. *Psychological practices with the physically disabled*. New York: Columbia University, 1962.

Lofquist, L. H., Siess, T. F., Dawis, R. V., England, G. W., & Weiss, D. J. Disability and work. *Minnesota Studies in Vocational Rehabilitation*, XVII, 1964.

National Council on Rehabilitation. *Symposium report*. New York: National Council on Rehabilitation, 1942.

Rusk, H. A. *Rehabilitation medicine*. St. Louis: Mosby, 1958.

Scott, I. D. *Manual of advisement and guidance*. Washington: U.S. Government Printing Office, 1945.

Wright, B. A. *Physical disability—a psychological approach*. New York: Harper, 1960.

8

Application
of the Theory

THE MAJOR VEHICLE FOR APPLYING THE THEORY OF WORK Adjustment is the professional practice of vocational counseling. In adjusting to work, an agent of adjustment (the vocational counselor) is suggested as the person who has the knowledge and techniques needed to assist an individual in learning about his work personality and about the characteristics of the available work environments. We are here suggesting that the same kind of counseling will be appropriate for the various social problem areas we have discussed (retirement, unemployment, disability). The long range criteria are work adjustment, and post-work adjustment in the case of retirement. The most reasonable data for the description, prediction, and achievement of these criteria are those that describe (in the same or in comparable terms) the work personality, the work environment, the educational environment, and the social environment.

To be sure, school counselors, college counselors, employment counselors, rehabilitation counselors, and retirement counselors work in different settings. They may require additional and special overlays of knowledge, such as knowledge of disabilities or of curricula, but the long-range goals of all these counselors, and the tools relevant to the achievement of these goals, are very similar indeed.

Vocational counseling practice in the context of the Theory of

Work Adjustment requires the vocational counselor to be expert in a number of ways. He must know how to measure the abilities and needs of individuals. He must be able to locate and interpret information which describes the ability requirements and the reinforcer systems of jobs; in other words, he must understand work environments in work-personality terms. He must view individuals in terms predictive of their work adjustment and must be able to communicate this knowledge to counselees, so that vocational decisions are made consonant with work adjustment potential.

Since discussions of counseling frequently focus almost completely on the important communication and relationship aspects of the counseling process, we will be concerned here only with what it is that needs to be communicated. Our concern, then, is with the data that describe work personalities and work environments, and that facilitate the prediction of work adjustment. Such data allow us to assess an individual's potential for work (vocational diagnosis) and to specify the job conditions necessary for his work adjustment (vocational prognosis).

If the vocational counselor is to operate in the manner described above, it will be necessary for vocational psychology to make available to him (as part of his research underpinnings) a great deal of additional carefully derived information about the ability requirements and the reinforcer systems of jobs, representing the entire range of job families. Vocational psychology must intensify its efforts in the area of measurement problems and should adopt as a major research problem the discovery, definition, and measurement of abilities and needs which will account for individual differences in responding to the full range of job requirements and reinforcer systems. In short, while vocational counselors now have many effective tools, they need better ones; they need many more empirically derived occupational ability patterns, and the information that would derive from the inclusion of procedures for determining and describing occupational reinforcer patterns as a part of routine and continuous job-analysis activity.

In industrial personnel work, or in vocational counseling with employed persons, the framework of the Theory of Work Adjustment should facilitate the determination of reasons for lack of satisfactoriness and/or satisfaction. It should also be useful in evaluating the effects of sudden changes in the individual (physical or emotional) or in the job (changes in duties, technological change, new policies, restrictions, and the like).

For the education of vocational counselors the theory has implications which center on the inclusion of a substantial subject matter dealing with occupations or work environments (the measurement and interpretation of ability requirements and reinforcer systems, and the commonalities for these across levels and fields of work), and dealing with individual vocational analysis (the measurement and interpretation of abilities and needs in describing the work personality). The theory argues for the importance of considerable emphasis on such subject matter while, of course, recognizing the importance of training for the communication and relationship aspects of counseling. The counselor does have to know how to maintain a relationship with his client, and how to facilitate counselee selection of jobs for which work adjustment is predicted. He must know how to use such tools as reinforcement, environmental manipulation, and occupational information. While recognizing the value of catharsis (as the counselee is assisted in freeing himself of some of his emotional problems), counselor education based on the Theory of Work Adjustment would not rely solely on this approach, or even assume that such an approach is either necessary or effective with many counselees whose problems center on work.

The theory also suggests less emphasis in counselor education and counseling practice on group labels ("over-dependency of counselees," "anxiety") and more emphasis on individual work personality–work environment relationships (the utilization of abilities and the satisfaction of needs).

The theory further suggests that the appropriate focus is *not* on changing the counselee to fit the world of work. Perhaps some minimum change is feasible in a relatively short counseling relationship. The theory does suggest, however, that relatively little change (except for persons with very limited response repertoires and/or reinforcement histories) is likely. Assuming that large numbers of our population have relatively "normal" work personalities the appropriate emphasis for vocational counseling is placed on finding appropriate situations in the realities of the world of work in which a counselee can utilize his abilities and satisfy his needs. For example, instead of working to reduce client dependency (in a client who is not immobilized by the presence of this trait) or seeking to increase problem solving ability (in a client with a long history of behavioral experience with problem solving) the counselor seeks to help the counselee to find appropriate work environments to which he can adjust with his established work personality. He takes the "normal" counselee as he is and tries to help him to capitalize on his work personality, not change its characteristics.

Using the Theory of Work Adjustment as the basis for conceptualizing vocational counseling, the following specific procedures are suggested.

1. The counselor should obtain information enabling him to estimate the counselee's needs in order to facilitate management of the initial stages of counseling. Some knowledge of counselee needs will help the counselor to structure his plan for establishing a continuing relationship. For example, if data indicate a strong dependency need, the counselor might take a more active role in leading the interview. In the present state of practice, the counselor must infer counselee needs from such data sources as school cumulative records, referral information from agency workers, available test results, other records, and correspondence with the counselee. The important considerations are that the counselor have a systematic conceptualization of needs; that he view data in terms of this conceptualization; and that he test his inferences about needs in his initial interviews with the counselee.

When the technology of counseling is improved, perhaps the counselor will have available to him a referral instrument designed to include those data shown by research to be significantly related to measured needs. With such an instrument he should be able to make (with varying degrees of confidence) inferences about the needs of a specific counselee. The referral instrument might provide the basis for the initial interview; that is, it could be used as an "intake instrument." Some research (Warnken & Siess, 1965) indicates that such an instrument could be developed. Given a systematic conceptualization of needs, and an instrument to measure needs, it would be possible to select items for a referral instrument, with an approach similar to that used in developing weighted application blanks (England, 1961).

There is certainly no reason why the counselor must wait upon the completion of such research and the validation of such an instrument. By way of an interim measure, he should examine the data accessible to him, select and group data from the counselee histories likely to be related to needs, and design a referral instrument which facilitates the assessment of needs from these data. He should verify assessments based on such an instrument against actual need measurements taken later in the counseling process.

2. In the first interviews, the counselee should be encouraged to express fully his vocational and other problems, his aspirations, and his understanding of his possibilities for working with his problems and aspirations. This procedure should provide some verification of the counselor's initial estimate of the counselee's needs. It also should provide reference points against which subsequent measurements may be evaluated to ascertain the extent of the counselee's knowledge of his work personality and of his potentialities in the world of work. This type of information helps to identify for the counselor the optimal beginning steps in the counseling process, and defines the areas of information in which he must communicate most effectively with this counselee.

3. The counselor should obtain extensive personal history data from the counselee, including educational, social, and work-history information. These data are needed to provide a context within which the initial referral data and the counselee's statements of his problems and aspirations can be viewed. These data will serve also as a background for subsequent psychometric evaluation. Because personal history data reflect an individual's reinforcement history the counselor will be able to improve his initial estimates of counselee needs in the course of gathering these data. He will also gain information about the general intelligence level of the counselee and this information will aid him in choosing the appropriate instruments for use in psychometric evaluation.

4. The counselor should obtain data which will establish the counselee's present levels of abilities and needs. The most accurate and most dependable means for obtaining these data are provided

by psychometric evaluation. Using testing procedures, the counselor samples the broad range of measurable abilities and needs so that he can describe the counselee's unique work personality. The counselor's earlier estimates of his counselee's needs will guide the manner in which he introduces and carries out this psychometric evaluation. While personal history data are useful in establishing the counselee's abilities and needs, psychometric data are preferable because work environments are more readily and more frequently described in psychometric terms. The counselor will find personal history data useful in corroborating test results. Discrepancies between personal history and test-derived data will point to areas requiring further assessment of the work personality.

In the present state of vocational psychology the counselor has available to him instruments to measure a wide variety of abilities. However, his choice of instruments is limited by the extent to which they have also been used to describe various work environments. In some cases—for example, in the development and standardization of multifactor tests such as the General Aptitude Test Battery (Dvorak, 1956) and the Differential Aptitude Tests (Bennett et al., 1947–1959)—the individual and the environment (work and/or educational) have been measured using the same set of dimensions.

In the area of need measurement (as needs are defined in the Theory of Work Adjustment) the counselor does not have as wide a selection of instruments. Some beginnings have been made in the measurement of work-relevant needs (Super, 1962, 1964; Weiss et al., 1964), and in the description of the work environment on the same dimensions (Weiss et al., 1965). Until recently, the counselor has had to infer the work-relevant need patterns of the counselee from interest and personality measurements, using established instruments (such as the Strong Vocational Interest Blank, the Kuder Preference Record, the Minnesota Vocational Interest Inventory, the Minnesota Multiphasic Personality Inventory, the Edwards Personal Preference Schedule, and the Allport-Vernon-Lindzey Study of Values). In order to relate these inferred patterns to the work environment he had to utilize the available information on job reinforcer systems (such as the temperament ratings found in the *Worker Trait Requirements for 4,000 Jobs,* the

Dictionary of Occupational Titles, or in other published job descriptions). The Work Adjustment Project at the University of Minnesota has approached these problems more directly. It has now developed one measure of work-relevant needs (the Minnesota Importance Questionnaire; see Appendix). It also has developed a considerable number of ORP's which describe occupations in terms of reinforcers for the same set of needs (see Appendix for an example; Borgen et al., 1968).

Much research is yet to be done on the discovery, definition, and measurement of ability and need dimensions which will account for individual differences in responding to the full range of job requirements and reinforcer systems. This research area should be given the highest priority in vocational psychology.

5. The counselor should determine a number of occupational possibilities for the counselee. He does this by collating his extensive psychometric information about the counselee's work personality with similar information about the available work environments. One way in which the counselor can accomplish this task is by determining the following: a) which jobs, across levels and fields of work, are similar in ability requirements and reinforcer systems to the counselee's stabilized abilities and needs (in other words, the counselor must examine information on the OAP's and ORP's for a representative number of jobs); b) which jobs (in terms of their OAP's and ORP's) correspond optimally to the counselee's work personality (in terms of his abilities and needs).

If this task of matching men and jobs is to be carried out in the most effective manner, more work must be done to further the development of OAP and ORP descriptions of jobs. In order to be most useful to the counselor this information must be organized so that fields and levels of work are represented and so that the job groupings are based on similarities in OAP and ORP characteristics regardless of field and level classifications. Obviously, because of the large number of jobs involved, the development and use of this information will require extensive use of electronic data processing techniques. Furthermore, improved techniques for determining degrees of matching that will predict satisfactoriness and satisfaction for specific jobs must be developed. The validation of the Theory of Work Adjustment requires the development of such techniques. In the present state of technology, counselors use matching methods to predict job success. However, their activity is limited by the kinds of prediction tables available, by the lack of systematic organization of such prediction tables, and by the limited use of work-adjustment criteria (measures of both satisfactoriness and satisfaction) in research on the prediction of job success.

6. Utilizing his knowledge of the counselee's response and reinforcement history, the counselor should attempt to bring about vocational choices for which the ability and need correspondences with work-environment characteristics are such that work adjustment can be predicted. The counselor may seek to facilitate appropriate vocational decisions by means of such techniques as reinforcement in the interview, the use of occupational information, and the placement of the counselee in reinforcing work-relevant situations. It is understood that these techniques are aimed at facilitating vocational choices which will insure work adjustment and its attendant satisfaction for the counselee and satisfactoriness for the employer and society.

7. The counselor should, as a matter of course, follow up on the outcomes of his predictions concerning each counselee's work adjustment. This should provide the counselor with a source of data to be used in evaluating and improving his methods of prediction.

The procedures described above constitute the basic and minimum requirements for vocational counseling based on the Theory of Work Adjustment. It is recognized that the practice of vocational counseling in different settings and with different counselee populations will require the addition of specialized knowledge and techniques to this basic set of procedures.

The vocational counselor in the school setting may be immediately concerned with the prediction of success in educational and training programs. He also will be working with younger counselees whose work personalities may not have reached a stable stage of development. Therefore, in addition to the knowledge and techniques required for carrying out the basic counseling procedures, he should have specialized knowledge of psychological tests and other assessment devices for the age group with which he is working. He must also be well informed about the requirements and reinforcements in educational and training environments. However, it must be emphasized that, while measures of success in educational and training programs are important intermediate criteria, their long-range significance lies in their relevance to the more fundamental criteria of work adjustment. Similar considerations would be appropriate for vocational counseling carried out in a college setting.

The vocational rehabilitation counselor must concern himself with the effects of disabling conditions (illnesses or injuries). In addition to the knowledge and techniques included in basic counseling procedures, he should have specialized knowledge of medical information in order to communicate with medical and related specialists. He should also be well informed about the plans for medical treatment and about the physician's recommendations for counselee activity. He also will want to have specialized knowledge of the training and rehabilitation facilities that are available to disabled individuals.

While the vocational rehabilitation counselor is expected to have these kinds of specialized information, the Theory of Work Adjustment requires that he assess the *impact* of disabling conditions on the counselee using work-adjustment measures (in terms of ability loss and associated changes in needs) rather than view his counselee as belonging to a medical category with stereotypic expectations for him as a member of that group. In order to make this psychometric assessment he must be able to reconstruct the counselee's work personality prior to the disabling condition using the types of data generally available in school, agency, and industrial records.

While the focus here is placed on vocational rehabilitation counseling for work adjustment, it is recognized that these counselors also need knowledge and skills to work with the initial emotional impact of the disabling condition on counselees. Even in this stage of rehabilitation counseling, knowledge of the work personality prior to the disabling condition would appear to be essential in objectively determining the actual impact and in assessing the counselee's subjective reactions. A more complete discussion of this approach is contained in Lofquist et al. (1964).

Retirement counselors should be able to utilize the basic vocational counseling procedures suggested by the Theory of Work

Adjustment. In addition they will need special competence and knowledge to view social environments and recreational activities in adjustment terms. That is, they will wish to describe these environments in terms of their ability requirements and their reinforcer systems. They will also wish to determine what remains of the work environment for the retired individual that will continue to contribute to his over-all adjustment. The retirement counselor should focus on utilizing the individual's work personality in a changed environment, rather than on changing the individual's abilities and needs.

The employment counselor represents the group of practitioners for which the basic counseling procedures suggested by the theory are most effective with little addition of specialized knowledge and techniques. However, these counselors often work with counselee groups whose work personalities are likely to be less differentiated than those of the general working population. These counselees may be younger, lacking in work experience, chronically unemployed, generally employed at the unskilled level, from minority groups, or from low socioeconomic levels. They may show potentialities rather than actual developed abilities. These counselees may also have had limited experiences with reinforcers. The employment counselor, therefore, may require special skills, knowledge, and resources to enable him to identify emerging abilities and to enlarge his counselees' experiences with reinforcers related to work. It is obvious that more research is urgently needed to facilitate the effectiveness of the employment counselor so that he may focus on individualized work adjustment.

References

Bennett, G. K., Seashore, H. G., & Wesman, A. G. *Differential aptitude tests.* New York: Psychological Corporation, 1957-1959.

Borgen, F. H., Weiss, D. J., Tinsley, H. E. A., Dawis, R. V., & Lofquist, L. H. Occupational Reinforcer Patterns. *Minnesota Studies in Vocational Rehabilitation,* XXIV, 1968.

Dvorak, B. J. The general aptitude test battery. *Personnel and Guidance Journal,* 1956, *35*, 145-154.

England, G. W. *Development and use of weighted application blanks.* Dubuque: Brown, 1961.

Lofquist, L. H., Siess, T. F., Dawis, R. V., England, G. W., & Weiss, D. J. Disability and work. *Minnesota Studies in Vocational Rehabilitation,* XVII, 1964.

Super, D. E. The structure of work values in relation to status, achievement, interests, and adjustment. *Journal of Applied Psychology,* 1962, *42,* 231-239.

Super, D. E. *Work values inventory form 1.* New York: Teachers College, Columbia University, 1964.

Warnken, R. G., & Siess, T. F. The use of the cumulative record in the prediction of behavior. *Personnel and Guidance Journal,* 1965, *44,* 231-237.

Weiss, D. J., Dawis, R. V., England, G. W., & Lofquist, L. H. The measurement of vocational needs. *Minnesota Studies in Vocational Rehabilitation,* XVI, 1964.

Weiss, D. J., Dawis, R. V., England, G. W., & Lofquist, L. H. An inferential approach to occupational reinforcement. *Minnesota Studies in Vocational Rehabilitation,* XIX, 1965.

9

Meeting
Manpower Needs

MUCH OF THE LEGISLATIVE EFFORT IN THE "GREAT SOCIETY" programs was directed towards such goals as employment for the hard core unemployed, equal opportunity for work, training minority group members for work, upgrading individuals' job skills, increasing work opportunities in disadvantageous labor market areas, relocating workers to more viable labor markets, counseling youth for work, helping individuals to adjust to leaving the labor force for retirement, and providing general and special education that will, among other things, facilitate productive and satisfying employment. Prior to the great society programs, there were a number of other programs (with similar work-adjustment kinds of goals) such as the vocational rehabilitation program for physically and emotionally disabled individuals, the counseling and training programs for returning servicemen and disabled veterans, the program for training school counselors to work in our secondary schools, and the federal-state employment service program to provide counseling and placement for any citizen. These examples make the obvious point that there is a great deal of legislation in effect that specifies or implies long-range goals in the general category of adjustment to work.

Often the legislation itself and the discussion that shapes it and facilitates its passage correctly point out the importance of work to complete the satisfaction and insure the dignity of any man. In addition, a man's worth as a producing economic unit and his ability after job placement to repay the cost of specific legislation in a short span of years are considered. The arguments for social legislation to facilitate work adjustment, and the social and economic benefits likely to accompany it, are compelling for both the legislative branch and the public. Whenever such legislation has been passed and funded, there has been an urgent demand for agencies and administrators to start service programs immediately. Substantial results have then been expected by the end of the fiscal year.

The kinds of programs we are discussing either specify or imply that the individuals to be served will be assisted in making their adjustments to work and their choices of jobs by professional counselors educated to serve as vocational experts. Some programs include job titles and brief descriptions of the kinds of counselors who are to be employed. Not much attention is given, however, to specific job duties that will insure utilization of the existing technology in vocational psychology, nor to the likelihood of filling the newly created positions with qualified professional manpower. It is worth noting that of the social programs directed towards work adjustment that are mentioned above, only the vocational rehabilitation, veterans rehabilitation, and secondary-school counselor programs have been concerned enough with the supply of qualified personnel to have also initiated and maintained counselor-education programs to insure that practice will meet professional standards in vocational counseling. Even these programs, however, can no longer meet current staffing needs. The expansion of existing service programs and the demands of new programs make the number of vocational counselors who will be trained in the forseeable future look very inadequate indeed.

The need for specially educated vocational counselors has far outrun the present and the anticipated supply. It is a fact that we cannot adequately staff either the established or the recently legislated programs. Harried administrators who must get programs under way are sometimes tempted to hire less qualified staff and to train them later. They take the "advice" to forget about the "old technology" and to "innovate" and thus get programs under way, but they usually find it difficult to arrange further training for staff, and perhaps find it even more difficult to "innovate."

In any case these actions are distressing to vocational psychologists and to counselor educators who work with the knowledge that there is a useful technology for practice, that there is a need to train additional qualified practitioners, and that there is a need to make maximum use of trained personnel.

Throughout this book we have discussed the complexities faced by an individual in adjusting to work. The conceptualization of work adjustment in the form of the Theory of Work Adjustment has implications for the practice of vocational counseling. It helps to delineate an existing technology that *is* available; it points up areas in the technology that require strengthening through additional research; and it enables one to describe specific practices to be followed in vocational counseling, where the goal is work adjustment. This conceptualization and the technology it represents makes it possible to develop a plan for meeting manpower needs.

The plan for meeting manpower needs requires a new approach that stresses three different points:

1. Three different levels of education beyond the bachelors degree, with different emphases, are necessary in the broad field of vocational psychology.

2. Counseling functions need to be job-analyzed and described with a new focus on levels of functioning.

3. Parts of the vocational counseling and agency administration procedures need to be mechanized and simplified to facilitate their use by personnel educated to function at different levels of competence.

The next several paragraphs will illustrate possible specific steps that can be taken to implement these three suggestions.

More individuals must be educated to the doctorate level of competence in vocational psychology and in its applied special area of vocational counseling psychology. Such education in vocational psychology should be aimed primarily at producing high-level research workers to improve the technology of work adjustment and to translate research findings into applied procedures of utility to professional personnel educated to less technical levels of competence. Doctorate level education in vocational counseling psychology should also have as its goal the expansion of high-level manpower available to teach vocational counseling in our graduate schools, and to direct agency programs and agency staff development and training. Legislation intended to facilitate work adjustment should provide for the establishment of faculties and student stipend programs in these areas and at this level of education.

Continuing educational programs at the masters level in vocational counseling need to be expanded in agencies where they exist (such as in the Rehabilitation Services Administration), and provided for in agencies where they do not exist (such as in the war on poverty programs and the federal-state employment service system). The point has already been made in Chapter 8 that perhaps there is a basis for a common training that has implications for practice across the special areas within vocational counseling psychology (rehabilitation, employment service, and school counseling). Since the total manpower needs for practicing vocational counselors appear unlikely to be met by masters-level programs, the primary aims of these educational programs are seen as providing counselor supervisors, and counselors who will work with more limited case loads of those clients for whom diagnosis, treatment, and communication problems are particularly difficult. A good deal of experience with government-sponsored training at this level is available and could be used effectively by agencies that might want to start training programs.

A third level of education can probably be successfully undertaken in the form of short-term training at colleges and universities with an emphasis on technological applications. This would be followed up by continuing in-service training programs within the service agencies themselves. Such training should be directed towards sub-masters-level practitioners who will utilize the technology developed and interpreted by vocational psychologists, and who will be supervised in both applications and case-load management by the masters-level vocational counselors. In order to make continuous progress in a program of in-service training, and to be assured of upward mobility (as a career incentive), individuals hired for training and practice at this level should, whenever possible, have the abilities that will enable them to pursue graduate-level education at a later date, if this becomes desirable.

For a general reserve of professional manpower to be established and a common pool of professional techniques to be developed, these three levels of education must be seen as interdependent in terms of goals and balance, and as operating across all major agencies (public and private) that deal in programs oriented towards work adjustment. This requires improved agency-university cooperation of the kind discussed in the McGowan report (1965). It also requires considerable study of the feasibility of coordinating activities in the several independent major agencies concerned with helping people to adjust in work. Perhaps we are at the point in time where it is necessary to suggest that a national high-level coordinator of vocational counseling practices be appointed in consultation with the professional communities in vocational psychology and counseling psychology, and the practicing agencies, and who will have authority to function across agencies. This suggestion arises from the current state of confusion that characterizes our approaches to meeting public needs through vocational counseling. Agencies are understaffed and, in many cases, have underqualified personnel. Agencies compete with each other for qualified staff only to find them in very short supply. Colleges and universities, in the midst of facing the demands of a markedly expanded student population, find it difficult to provide sufficient faculty for the expanding graduate-level educational programs and the in-service training programs requested by agencies. Agencies and universities alike appear on the surface to be uncooperative. Both the hiring of substandard personnel by the agencies and the lack of ability to educate more fully trained personnel by the universities are to be deplored. Professional organizations are concerned about the effects of new social legislation on the accepted standards for professional preparation (the masters level is the minimum for practicing vocational-educational counselors). It is obvious that the legislation of new positions and the provision of funds for these positions will not in themselves solve our current problems. It is necessary to define the desired levels of education and to support these as one part of an approach to the manpower problem.

To employ a levels-of-education approach effectively, however, it is necessary to do a careful job analysis of vocational counseling functions and to group functions by levels. Most counseling psy-

chologists would agree that there are several job requirements
that they meet frequently that *do not* call upon skills and knowledge provided by their high level of education (at either the
masters or the doctorate level). In conjunction with job analysis
activity, it is desirable to simplify the tools available and to organize the methods of using them. Some tools and procedures now
employed only by highly trained personnel can be mechanized so
that they can be applied competently by less trained persons. In
the following paragraphs we will attempt to illustrate the ways in
which vocational counseling could be organized to utilize personnel
educated for different levels of competence.

Agencies can set up systems for procuring relevant advance
referral information on clients to be seen for service. Such information can be obtained from typical referral sources, from the clients
themselves, and from social institutions known typically to have
served the agencies' clients (such as schools or the employment
service). The relevance of such information for screening and for
client assignment to personnel in the agency would be determined
by vocational psychologists with research competency. Structured
referral information forms can be prepared that will specify the
minimum information needed. Different combinations of information can be used to indicate whether or not an agency can be of
service, what services are likely to be most effective, what level
of counseling difficulty is likely, what extent of agency involvement
is necessary, and how the client is likely to react in his first con-
tacts with the agency (see Chapter 8).

Using such a system, a masters-level supervisor or an agency-
office supervisor can specify in advance the data to be checked,
the hypotheses to be explored, the likely courses of action, and,
in many cases, the rather simple actions necessary to resolve
problems. With the advance referral information and the supervisor's recommendations, clients can be seen for initial interviews
by an intake interviewer. There is no reason why these intake
interviewers would require training beyond the baccalaureate
level if they function under competent supervision and in a system
of systematic review. Sensitive and reliable individuals with some
in-service training in effective interpersonal relations should be
able to meet the job requirements.

Intake interviewers should be able to describe agency functions, answer requests for relatively simple information, refer those clients who cannot be served to other agencies, and arrange referrals within the agency to higher professional staff levels. The intake interviewer obviously must function under the supervision of a qualified vocational counselor.

Another level of professional personnel at the sub-masters level but with considerable in-service training (conducted by doctorate- and masters-level persons) should be able to do much of what the masters-level vocational counselor now does. To make this feasible, however, we must translate our techniques into forms that make applications simpler, and perhaps even more effective, than they are at the present time. We must also insure continuous supervision by counselors educated to the level of present standards (the masters degree, usually requiring two years of graduate work).

A brief description of a program of testing being carried out by the Minnesota Work Adjustment Project with the Minnesota Division of Vocational Rehabilitation may illustrate how counseling can be aided by modern technology. The testing program is set up primarily to gather research data, but has implications for counselor functioning and for counselor in-service training.

First, let us assume that fully trained counselors choose tests most useful for a client population to be served from a considerable knowledge of the validities, reliabilities, and applicability of test information for understanding both the individual's work personality and the work environment. Such counselors are accustomed to using data presented in such forms as standard scores, prediction tables, or expectancy tables. In addition they are familiar with such tools as occupational ability patterns and with the need-satisfying properties of various kinds of work. They know where to find the necessary resource materials. They also often give tests themselves, spending a perhaps unwarranted amount of professional time in clerical-administrative work.

In the Work Adjustment Project testing program, all clients referred to the state rehabilitation agency are tested by psychometricians on a predetermined battery of the most relevant tests. This battery can of course be supplemented by additional testing later in the counseling process. The client takes the General Aptitude Test Battery (GATB), the Minnesota Vocational Interest Inventory, the Minnesota Importance Questionnaire, the

Minnesota Multiphasic Personality Inventory, and the Strong Vocational Interest Blank (if the client is a high school graduate). The following treatment of the test data illustrates both mechanization and the focusing of counseling in directions that utilize accepted tools and procedures. Only the GATB results will be discussed here.

For each individual, the GATB is scored on a computer and processed through a program that prints out raw scores, standard scores, percentiles for each subtest, and the OAP's for which this individual qualifies. This leads the counselor to a list of possible jobs for each OAP for which the individual meets minimal ability requirements. In addition the program prints out the page and line numbers that correspond to job titles in the *Worker Trait Requirements for 4,000 Jobs* (WTR) for all of the listed jobs for which the individual's abilities qualify him. This leads the counselor to additional essential information, such as that pertaining to levels of education (general and special), interests, temperaments, and physical requirements that are deemed by job analysts to be desirable for job success. Finally, the print-out shows that the individual has the requisite abilities to perform on specific jobs. Figure 7 shows the computer output for an actual client.

With the recent development of ORP's for specific occupations, it is now also feasible to compare an individual's measured work-relevant needs with the reinforcer characteristics of a variety of occupations. The computer can compare needs and reinforcers for those jobs for which the individual already has been shown to meet minimal ability requirements. This would reduce the number of appropriate jobs shown in the example in Figure 7.

Information presented in this way saves time in testing, scoring, interpreting, and locating the most relevant resource information. Methods like this facilitate the use of relevant but simply presented data on clients by less skilled persons working under supervision, freeing masters-level personnel to use their higher levels of skill in supervision, training, case planning, and working with those clients whose problems are extremely complicated.

The work by Gilbert and Ewing (1964) illustrates another application of modern technology which may add to the sophistication of vocational counseling practice. With the use of programmed instruction techniques in test interpretation, counselor

Figure 7. Computer Print-Out of GATB Scores and Related OAP's

CASE NUMBER—103530   DATE—17 NOV 66

SCORES ON THE GENERAL APTITUDE TEST BATTERY (GATB)

	STANDARD SCORE	PERCENTILE	WTR CODE
G—GENERAL LEARNING ABILITY	76	12	4
V—VERBAL ABILITY	80	16	4
N—NUMERICAL ABILITY	86	25	4
S—SPATIAL ABILITY	74	10	5
P—FORM PERCEPTION	87	26	4
Q—CLERICAL PERCEPTION	103	56	3
K—MOTOR COORDINATION	109	67	2
F—FINGER DEXTERITY	85	23	4
M—MANUAL DEXTERITY	83	20	4

ON THE BASIS OF GATB SCORES, THE INDIVIDUAL QUALIFIES
FOR THE FOLLOWING OAP PATTERNS—22 31 32 35

THE GATB SCORES OF THIS INDIVIDUAL EQUAL OR EXCEED THE WORKER TRAIT REQUIREMENTS
ESTIMATES FOR THE FOLLOWING JOBS

Figure 8. Sample Print-Out for Work Assignment Sheet

CASE NUMBER	ALPHANUMERIC	NAME	STATUS	TYPE	REVIEW	FLAG
268	2	KJONES				HAS BEEN IN STATUS ZERO FOR MORE THAN 3 MONTHS. CHECK CASE FILE FOR EYE REPORT, MEDICAL REPORT, AND SOCIAL HISTORY. REQUEST NEEDED INFORMATION OR ACCOMPLISH PROCESSING.
274	239	GSMITH	2	1	YES	
1294	391	MPETERS	5	1	YES	1. HAS THE TRAINING PROGRAM RUN ITS COURSE. 2. IS AN AMENDMENT OR ANY CURRENT SERVICE CONSIDERED NECESSARY. 3. WOULD YOU PREDICT THIS CASE WILL CONTINUE IN ITS NORMAL PROGRESSION. IF THE ANSWER IS NO TO NUMBER 3, THIS CASE NEEDS FURTHER DISCUSSION AND A SPECIAL TREATMENT PLAN.
3000	8	LDOBBIN	7	1	—	CONTACT

4000 MGREEN 1 1 YES

1. HAS THIS CASE HAD UNUSUAL PROBLEMS THAT HAVE DELAYED ITS PROGRESS.
2. IS A PLAN BEING DEVELOPED THAT WILL BE READY WITHIN THREE MONTHS.
3. CAN WE EXPECT PROGRESSION THROUGH 12.
IF THE ANSWER TO 3 IS NO, THIS CASE SHOULD BE DISCUSSED FOR POSSIBLE CLOS-
ING FOR OTHER REASONS.

735 GBROWN 6 1 YES

1. IS THIS CLIENT STILL READY FOR EMPLOYMENT.
2. IS THERE EVIDENCE SHOWING CLIENT IS LIKELY TO BE EMPLOYED.
3. WOULD YOU PREDICT ACTUAL EMPLOYMENT IN THREE MONTHS WITHOUT OUR
INTERVENTION.
IF THE ANSWER IS NO, CASE NEEDS FURTHER DISCUSSION.

365 LBURTON 8 1 YES

1. IS A NEW PLAN BEING DEVELOPED ON THIS CASE.
2. CAN WE PREDICT THAT THIS CLIENT CAN BE RETURNED TO PREVIOUS CATE-
GORY BEFORE ANOTHER REVIEW.
3. SHOULD THIS CASE BE CLOSED FOR OTHER REASONS AFTER PLAN.

691 KPETERSON 1 2 YES

382 KANDERS COUNSELOR DID NOT SPECIFY FREQUENCY
OF REVIEW.

time can be saved for use in the more critical parts of the vocational counseling process; programmed interpretation can be presented in the counseling process by less skilled personnel (after vocational psychologists have programmed the material); and clients will receive a clear understanding of their assets and liabilities through this process.

Mechanization can also be effectively employed at the administrative level. For example, Weiss and Potter (1965), working with the Minnesota Work Adjustment Project, developed a computer-based system of record keeping for the State Services for the Blind in Minnesota. After evaluating the data to be included and examining the data-reporting structure of the agency, they set up a program which prints out information on the status of case actions at regular intervals. This print-out enables supervisors and counselors to keep up with the demands of heavy case loads and appears to motivate efficient case handling as well as appropriate data gathering. Figure 8 shows a page of the print-out for a counselor's case load. The program also prints out total agency report data whenever this is desired. An annual report is printed out in a few minutes and requires only the dictation of the verbal context in which the data are to be presented.

The use of such administrative technology in combination with simplified data-processing and data-presentation techniques in counseling should facilitate better agency use of manpower skills in a tight professional labor market.

The brief examples discussed above point to the possibility of changing our traditional vocational counseling procedures so that we can make better use of professional personnel at different levels of education. If we also improve our technology by increasing research in vocational psychology, we may become more effective in facilitating the work adjustment of individuals.

References

Gilbert, W. M., & Ewing, T. N. Counseling by teaching machine procedures. Paper read at the 1964 meetings of the American Psychological Association.

McGowan, J. F. (Ed.) *Counselor development in American society*. Conference recommendations from invitational conference on government-university relations in the professional preparation and employment of counselors, 1965.

Weiss, D. J., & Potter, C. S. Electronic data processing and state agency operations. Unpublished study, Work Adjustment Project, University of Minnesota, 1965 (mimeographed).

Weiss, D. J., Dawis, R. V., England, G. W., & Lofquist, L. H. An inferential approach to occupational reinforcement. *Minnesota Studies in Vocational Rehabilitation,* XIX, 1965.

10

Summary

We LIVE IN A SOCIETY WHICH PLACES A HIGH VALUE ON WORK. Men are expected to come to terms with the requirements and the conditions of work. The study of man's relationship to work, and of the problems he faces in adjusting to work, should therefore have high priority.

Man has inherited a cultural view of work that gives it a central position in his life. He is expected to give work this central focus. Ideally he is free to choose the kind of work he wants to do, but actually his choices are limited by our social mores and by his own history. Social pressures dictate certain expectations about the work he will do, and his unique personality, a product of his developmental history, defines what he can contribute to the world of work and what he can gain from it.

The complexity of the world of work added to the complexity of each unique individual's personality make the achievement of work adjustment a very difficult task. Most individuals should have professional assistance in this task. At the present time such assistance is greatly limited by the state of the scientific technology available to practitioners. The practice of vocational counseling suffers from the lack of a systematic psychology of work which provides ways in which to conceptualize the problems of work and ways by which these problems may be resolved.

This volume is written as a contribution to the development of a psychology of work. It elaborates on the Theory of Work Adjustment, published by Dawis, et al. (1964, 1968), and uses it as a framework for viewing contemporary social problems related to work. This theoretical approach also points to the ways in which vocational psychology should be developed if it is to provide a better basis for the practice of vocational counseling.

Work adjustment is a process of interaction between an individual and his work environment. It is reflected in an individual's satisfaction and his satisfactoriness. An individual's satisfaction derives from his evaluation of the extent to which his needs are met in the work setting. His satisfactoriness is the evaluation by his employer, and by society, of his work behavior. The theory postulates that work adjustment can be predicted from a knowledge of the individual's work personality and the work environment.

According to the theory an individual's work personality is adequately described by his abilities and his needs. It is also possible to describe the work environment in terms of abilities required for satisfactory work performance, and the needs that are satisfiable by the work conditions. Such description makes it possible to evaluate the correspondence of work personalities and work environments. Satisfactoriness results from the correspondence of the individual's abilities to the ability requirements of a job. Satisfaction results from the correspondence of the reinforcer system in a job and the individual's needs. Knowledge of the combined levels of satisfactoriness and satisfaction makes it possible to predict job tenure.

The research literature in vocational psychology and research being done in the University of Minnesota Work Adjustment Project indicate that the Theory of Work Adjustment is a viable and useful way of conceptualizing the problems of work. A good deal of additional research is needed for thorough testing of the implications of the theory.

Priorities for research should be given to the refinement of instruments for the measurement of abilities and needs, satisfaction and satisfactoriness, and to the description of the work environment in terms of its ability requirements and reinforcer systems. In addition, research must be undertaken to develop better ways of determining the optimal degrees of correspondence between work personalities and work environments that will predict work adjustment. What is needed is a revitalization of research in vocational psychology that will improve the technological base for the practice of vocational counseling.

The Theory of Work Adjustment, as a part of the developing psychology of work, provides a way of conceptualizing some of the major social problems we face today. Placement and retraining activities directed towards alleviating the unemployment problem should be undertaken on an individualized basis with proper regard for the correspondence between work personalities and work environments. The problems resulting from automation will be less of a threat if they are viewed in terms of individual job mobility, that is as problems of identifying those new jobs which have work-environment characteristics that are suited to an individual's work personality. Retirement can be viewed less in terms of the individual changing his style of life, and more in terms of identifying in the social environment and in the residual work environment those ability-requirement and reinforcer-system characteristics likely to facilitate personality-environment correspondences that in turn will promote adjustment. Disability would be viewed in terms of the implications of changes in an individual's work personality rather than almost exclusively in terms of the expectations for work that are associated with membership in a medically defined class. Attempts to deal with the problem of poverty should stress the utilization of each individual's abilities and the satisfaction of his needs rather than any change of his basic personality structure. If education is seen as the vehicle for the maximal development of each individual for adjustment to life, and if work is seen as a major portion of life, more attention should be directed towards the structuring of educational environments to facilitate the maximal development of work personalities by providing for experience with a wide range of requirement-reinforcer conditions found in work.

The practice of vocational counseling provides the major vehicle for applying the Theory of Work Adjustment to the several social problem areas mentioned above. Vocational counseling practice, viewed in the context of the theory, requires expertise in assessing work personalities and work environments, in predicting work adjustment from such assessment, and in communicating with counselees so that vocational decisions are made consonant with work adjustment potential. The theory places particular emphasis on finding appropriate situations in which the counselee can utilize his abilities and satisfy his needs in the world of work, *not* on changing the counselee to fit that world.

Specific procedures basic to the practice of vocational counseling in the context of the theory are described in Chapters 8 and 9. These procedures constitute the basic core of vocational counseling practice. Vocational counseling in specialized settings or with specialized populations will require the addition of specialized knowledge and techniques to this basic core.

Present legislation directed towards the solution of social problems specifies or implies work adjustment as a major goal. Implementation of this goal will require professional manpower far in excess of the current or anticipated supply. In its specification of both the knowledge and the techniques required for vocational counseling practice, the theory suggests that professional personnel can be educated to function at different levels of competence within specialized areas of the vocational counseling field. The correspondence model on which the theory is based lends itself to the use of computer methods to facilitate the presentation of complex data in a more simplified form. This in turn simplifies the educational requirements for first-line vocational counselors, permitting the more highly educated vocational counselors to function as supervisors, while counseling psychologists, educated to the highest level, are freed to contribute more extensively to teaching and research in vocational psychology.

Epilogue

This book would be incomplete if we neglected to remark that the correspondence model on which the Theory of Work Adjustment is based is easily generalized. Our professional interests lie in vocational psychology, and the focus of this book has been on adjustment to work. The general correspondence model, however, can be useful in the understanding and explanation of any problem involving the adjustment of individuals to their environments. What is involved basically is the description of environments and individuals in terms of the most relevant personality dimensions, especially abilities (response capabilities) and needs (reinforcement values). Examples of the applicability of the correspondence model to some specific problem areas have been referred to in Chapter 7. These examples include adjustment to the educational environment and to the post-work environment. It is interesting to speculate about a future world in which work may no longer be the central focus of human activity. In such a world there will still be a major focus of activity, which might be recreation, cultural activities, intellectual pursuits, or even space exploration, and the individual will still have to come to terms with an environment. We submit that understanding the problems of adjustment to this new world will be facilitated by a conceptualization similar to that which underlies the Theory of Work Adjustment.

The authors hope that this book may stimulate renewed attention to the scientific study of work. In any event the writing of this book, during a period of far-reaching social change and of soul-searching in counseling psychology, has been a stimulating experience.

Appendix

Appendix

minnesota satisfaction questionnaire

1967 Revision

Restricted: For Research Use Only

Do not write in these spaces

© Copyright, 1967
Industrial Relations Center
University of Minnesota

Confidential

*Your answers to the questions and all other information you give us
will be held in strictest confidence.*

Check one: ☐ Male   ☐ Female

How old were you on your last birthday?
- ☐ Less than 20
- ☐ 20-24
- ☐ 25-29
- ☐ 30-34
- ☐ 35-39
- ☐ 40-44
- ☐ 45-49
- ☐ 50-54
- ☐ 55-59
- ☐ 60-65
- ☐ 65 and over

Check the box representing the number of years of schooling you completed:
- ☐ Grade School
- ☐ High School
- ☐ Trade or Business School, or some college
- ☐ College
- ☐ Graduate or Professional School

What is your present job called?_____

How long have you been in your present job?
- ☐ less than 1 year
- ☐ 1 to 2 years
- ☐ 3 to 5 years
- ☐ 6 to 10 years
- ☐ more than 10 years

How long have you been with this company?
- ☐ less than 1 year
- ☐ 1 to 2 years
- ☐ 3 to 5 years
- ☐ 6 to 10 years
- ☐ more than 10 years

What would you call your usual occupation, profession, trade or line of work?

_____

How many years have you been in this line of work?
- ☐ less than 1 year
- ☐ 1 to 2 years
- ☐ 3 to 5 years
- ☐ 6 to 10 years
- ☐ 11 to 15 years
- ☐ 16 to 20 years
- ☐ 21 to 25 years
- ☐ 26 to 30 years
- ☐ more than 30 years

Check the box which best describes where you belong:
- ☐ Supervisory, including management
- ☐ Office Services
  - ☐ Salaried
  - ☐ Hourly
- ☐ Field Representatives
- ☐ Automotive
- ☐ Day Warehouse
- ☐ Night Warehouse
  - ☐ 2nd Shift
  - ☐ 3rd Shift
- ☐ Corporate Store employees

3

Directions

In this questionnaire we would like to find out how you feel about certain aspects of your **present job.** You answers and those of other people help us to understand how people feel about their jobs, what they like an dislike about their jobs.

On the following pages you will find statements about certain aspects of your **present job.**

• Read each statement carefully.

• Decide how you feel about the aspect of your job described by the statement.

  —Circle 1 if you are **not satisfied** (if that aspect is much poorer than you would like it to be).

  —Circle 2 if you are **only slightly satisfied** (if that aspect is not quite what you would like it to be).

  —Circle 3 if you are **satisfied** (if that aspect is what you would like it to be).

  —Circle 4 if you are **very satisfied** (if that aspect is even better than you expected it to be).

  —Circle 5 if you are **extremely satisfied** (if that aspect is much better than you hoped it could be).

• Be sure to keep the statement in mind when deciding **how you feel about that aspect of your job**

• Do this for **all** statements. Answer **every** item.

• **Do not turn back** to previous statements.

Be frank. Give a true picture of your feelings about your **present job.**

sk yourself: How **satisfied** am I with this aspect of my job?

means I am **not satisfied** (this aspect of my job is much poorer than I would like it to be).

means I am **only slightly satisfied** (this aspect of my job is not quite what I would like it to be).

means I am **satisfied** (this aspect of my job is what I would like it to be).

means I am **very satisfied** (this aspect of my job is even better than I expected it to be).

means I am **extremely satisfied** (this aspect of my job is much better than I hoped it could be).

n my present job, this is how I feel about . . .	For each statement circle a number.				
1. the chance to be active much of the time	1	2	3	4	5
2. the variety in my work	1	2	3	4	5
3. the policies and practices toward employees of this company	1	2	3	4	5
4. the chance to be responsible for planning my work	1	2	3	4	5
5. the opportunities for advancement on this job	1	2	3	4	5
6. the social position in the community that goes with the job	1	2	3	4	5
7. the technical "know-how" of my supervisor	1	2	3	4	5
8. the spirit of cooperation among my co-workers	1	2	3	4	5
9. the way I am noticed when I do a good job	1	2	3	4	5
10. being able to do the job without feeling it is morally wrong	1	2	3	4	5
11. the chance to work by myself	1	2	3	4	5
12. the chance to do the kind of work that I do best	1	2	3	4	5
13. the way my supervisor and I understand each other	1	2	3	4	5
14. being able to see the results of the work I do	1	2	3	4	5
15. the chance to have other workers look to me for direction	1	2	3	4	5
16. the working conditions (heating, lighting, ventilation, etc.) on this job	1	2	3	4	5
17. the amount of pay for the work I do	1	2	3	4	5
18. the chance to try out some of my own ideas	1	2	3	4	5
19. the chance to be of service to others	1	2	3	4	5
20. my job security	1	2	3	4	5
21. the chance to develop close friendships with my co-workers	1	2	3	4	5
22. the way my boss handles his men	1	2	3	4	5
23. the chance to do different things from time to time	1	2	3	4	5
24. company policies and the way in which they are administered	1	2	3	4	5
25. the chances of getting ahead on this job	1	2	3	4	5

Ask yourself: How **satisfied** am I with this aspect of my job?

1 means I am **not satisfied** (this aspect of my job is much poorer than I would like it to be).

2 means I am **only slightly satisfied** (this aspect of my job is not quite what I would like it to be).

3 means I am **satisfied** (this aspect of my job is what I would like it to be).

4 means I am **very satisfied** (this aspect of my job is even better than I expected it to be).

5 means I am **extremely satisfied** (this aspect of my job is much better than I hoped it could be).

On my present job, this is how I feel about . . .	For each statement circle a number.				
26. the way my job provides for a secure future	1	2	3	4	
27. the way I get full credit for the work I do	1	2	3	4	
28. the chance to be of service to people	1	2	3	4	
29. the chance to work alone on the job	1	2	3	4	
30. being able to do things that don't go against my religious beliefs	1	2	3	4	
31. the chance to make decisions on my own	1	2	3	4	
32. the chance to do new and original things on my own	1	2	3	4	
33. the chance to tell other workers how to do things	1	2	3	4	
34. being able to take pride in a job well done	1	2	3	4	
35. being able to do something much of the time	1	2	3	4	
36. the physical surroundings where I work	1	2	3	4	
37. the chance to be "somebody" in the community	1	2	3	4	5
38. the chance to do work that is well suited to my abilities	1	2	3	4	5
39. the chance to make as much money as my friends	1	2	3	4	5
40. the competence of my supervisor in making decisions	1	2	3	4	5
41. the chance to help people	1	2	3	4	5
42. the recognition I get for the work I do	1	2	3	4	5
43. being able to do something worthwhile	1	2	3	4	5
44. the way my job provides for steady employment	1	2	3	4	5
45. the way employees are informed about company policies	1	2	3	4	5
46. the routine of my work	1	2	3	4	5
47. the friendliness of my co-workers	1	2	3	4	5
48. the chance to try something different	1	2	3	4	5
49. the chance to "rub elbows" with important people	1	2	3	4	5
50. being able to stay busy	1	2	3	4	5

sk yourself: How **satisfied** am I with this aspect of my job?

means I am **not satisfied** (this aspect of my job is much poorer than I would like it to be).

means I am **only slightly satisfied** (this aspect of my job is not quite what I would like it to be).

means I am **satisfied** (this aspect of my job is what I would like it to be).

means I am **very satisfied** (this aspect of my job is even better than I expected it to be).

means I am **extremely satisfied** (this aspect of my job is much better than I hoped it could be).

n my present job, this is how I feel about . . .	For each statement circle a number.				
51. the chance to be alone on the job	1	2	3	4	5
52. being able to do things that don't go against my conscience	1	2	3	4	5
53. the chance to be responsible for the work of others	1	2	3	4	5
54. the pleasantness of the working conditions	1	2	3	4	5
55. the way promotions are given out on this job	1	2	3	4	5
56. the way my boss delegates work to others	1	2	3	4	5
57. the chance to supervise other people	1	2	3	4	5
58. how my pay compares with that for similar jobs in other companies	1	2	3	4	5
59. the way my boss backs his men up (with top management)	1	2	3	4	5
60. the chance to make use of my best abilities	1	2	3	4	5
61. the freedom to use my own judgment	1	2	3	4	5
62. the way they usually tell me when I do my job well	1	2	3	4	5
63. the chance to tell people what to do	1	2	3	4	5
64. the chance to do things for other people	1	2	3	4	5
65. how steady my job is	1	2	3	4	5
66. the way company policies are put into practice	1	2	3	4	5
67. the chance to develop new and better ways to do the job	1	2	3	4	5
68. the chance to be "on the go" all the time	1	2	3	4	5
69. the chance to do my best at all times	1	2	3	4	5
70. the chance to do things that don't harm other people	1	2	3	4	5
71. the way my co-workers are easy to make friends with	1	2	3	4	5
72. the way my boss takes care of complaints brought to him by his men	1	2	3	4	5
73. the chance to be important in the eyes of others	1	2	3	4	5
74. my pay and amount of work I do	1	2	3	4	5
75. the chances for advancement on this job	1	2	3	4	5

Ask yourself: How **satisfied** am I with this aspect of my job?

1 means I am **not satisfied** (this aspect of my job is much poorer than I would like it to be).

2 means I am **only slightly satisfied** (this aspect of my job is not quite what I would like it to be).

3 means I am **satisfied** (this aspect of my job is what I would like it to be).

4 means I am **very satisfied** (this aspect of my job is even better than I expected it to be).

5 means I am **extremely satisfied** (this aspect of my job is much better than I hoped it could be).

On my present job, this is how I feel about . . .	For each statement circle a number.				
76. the chance to do something that makes use of my abilities	1	2	3	4	
77. the chance to work independently of others	1	2	3	4	
78. the chance to do something different every day	1	2	3	4	
79. the physical working conditions of the job	1	2	3	4	
80. the way my boss trains his men	1	2	3	4	
81. the chance to tell others what to do	1	2	3	4	
82. the personal relationship between my boss and his men	1	2	3	4	
83. the chance to do many different things on the job	1	2	3	4	
84. how my pay compares with that of other workers	1	2	3	4	
85. the way my co-workers get along with each other	1	2	3	4	
86. the responsibility of my job	1	2	3	4	
87. the way the company treats its employees	1	2	3	4	
88. the chance to be of some small service to other people	1	2	3	4	5
89. the chance to try my own methods of doing the job	1	2	3	4	5
90. being able to keep busy all the time	1	2	3	4	5
91. the way my boss provides help on hard problems	1	2	3	4	5
92. the working conditions	1	2	3	4	5
93. the chance to make use of my abilities and skills	1	2	3	4	5
94. the praise I get for doing a good job	1	2	3	4	5
95. the feeling of accomplishment I get from the job	1	2	3	4	5
96. the way layoffs and transfers are avoided in my job	1	2	3	4	5
97. the chance to work away from others	1	2	3	4	5
98. the chance to do the job without feeling I am cheating anyone	1	2	3	4	5
99. the chance to have a definite place in the community	1	2	3	4	5
100. my chances for advancement	1	2	3	4	5

k yourself: How **satisfied** am I with this aspect of my job?

means I am **not satisfied** (this aspect of my job is much poorer than I would like it to be).

means I am **only slightly satisfied** (this aspect of my job is not quite what I would like it to be).

means I am **satisfied** (this aspect of my job is what I would like it to be).

means I am **very satisfied** (this aspect of my job is even better than I expected it to be).

means I am **extremely satisfied** (this aspect of my job is much better than I hoped it could be).

my present job, this is how I feel about . . .	For each statement circle a number.				
1. the chance to complete a task I started	1	2	3	4	5
2. the facilities and equipment in my work	1	2	3	4	5
3. the company's reputation for treating its customers fairly	1	2	3	4	5
4. being able to see how my work fits into the total operation of the company	1	2	3	4	5
5. the way the company has stated its goals	1	2	3	4	5
6. the chance to work for a very well-known company	1	2	3	4	5
7. being told how I'm doing	1	2	3	4	5
8. the employee recreation program	1	2	3	4	5
9. the pension plan	1	2	3	4	5
0. being informed of important events in the company	1	2	3	4	5
1. the way other departments cooperate with my department	1	2	3	4	5
2. the leadership provided by company management	1	2	3	4	5
3. the way I am being paid at present (hourly or salary)	1	2	3	4	5
4. my understanding of how my work is related to company goals	1	2	3	4	5
5. being told where I stand	1	2	3	4	5
6. being able to follow through on a task	1	2	3	4	5
7. the reputation of the company	1	2	3	4	5
8. being able to work for a company that is important in its field	1	2	3	4	5
9. having the facilities and equipment I prefer	1	2	3	4	5
0. my understanding of company goals	1	2	3	4	5
21. the company group life, accident, sickness, hospital and surgical insurance plan	1	2	3	4	5
2. the company profit sharing plan	1	2	3	4	5
23. being informed of company benefits	1	2	3	4	5
24. the spirit of cooperation among departments	1	2	3	4	5
25. the ability of company management to provide leadership	1	2	3	4	5

Ask yourself: How **satisfied** am I with this aspect of my job?

1 means I am **not satisfied** (this aspect of my job is much poorer than I would like it to be).

2 means I am **only slightly satisfied** (this aspect of my job is not quite what I would like it to be).

3 means I am **satisfied** (this aspect of my job is what I would like it to be).

4 means I am **very satisfied** (this aspect of my job is even better than I expected it to be).

5 means I am **extremely satisfied** (this aspect of my job is much better than I hoped it could be).

On my present job, this is how I feel about . . .

For each statement circle a number.

126. the way I have to figure my hours worked (time card)	1	2	3	4
127. the chance to complete one task before being assigned another	1	2	3	4
128. my understanding of how my work is related to the overall company operation	1	2	3	4
129. the position of the company in relation to its competitors	1	2	3	4
130. how clearly company goals are stated	1	2	3	4
131. the reputation of the company's product or service	1	2	3	4
132. being told what management thinks of my work	1	2	3	4
133. the facilities and equipment provided by the company	1	2	3	4
134. the company length-of-service 5-25 year award program	1	2	3	4
135. the company profit sharing plan as a retirement program	1	2	3	4
136. being informed of company plans for employee benefits	1	2	3	4
137. the support my department can expect from other departments	1	2	3	4
138. company management in its role as leader	1	2	3	4
139. how I compare with workers in other departments in the way I am being paid (hourly or salary)	1	2	3	4
140. how well company goals are spelled out	1	2	3	4
141. the facilities and equipment to do my job	1	2	3	4
142. being able to understand how my job is related to other jobs in the company	1	2	3	4
143. the company's reputation in the community	1	2	3	4
144. the chance to finish what I start	1	2	3	4
145. being able to work for an important company	1	2	3	4
146. the care with which my performance is evaluated	1	2	3	4
147. the company magazine "Super Valu Ink"	1	2	3	4
148. the company profit sharing plan as an incentive to stay with the company	1	2	3	4
149. being informed of company plans for the future	1	2	3	4
150. the teamwork among the departments	1	2	3	4

yourself: How **satisfied** am I with this aspect of my job?

means I am **not satisfied** (this aspect of my job is much poorer than I would like it to be).

means I am **only slightly satisfied** (this aspect of my job is not quite what I would like it to be).

means I am **satisfied** (this aspect of my job is what I would like it to be).

means I am **very satisfied** (this aspect of my job is even better than I expected it to be).

means I am **extremely satisfied** (this aspect of my job is much better than I hoped it could be).

my present job, this is how I feel about . . .	For each statement circle a number.				
1. the leadership potential in company management	1	2	3	4	5
2. the system of figuring time and overtime in this company	1	2	3	4	5
3. how my work fits into the total company picture	1	2	3	4	5
4. the company's image in the community	1	2	3	4	5
5. the chance to work for a company that is a recognized leader in its field	1	2	3	4	5
6. the quality of the facilities and equipment in my job	1	2	3	4	5
7. the chance to do an entire job by myself	1	2	3	4	5
8. my knowledge of company goals	1	2	3	4	5
9. the way my performance is evaluated	1	2	3	4	5
10. the company profit sharing plan as an incentive to do a better job	1	2	3	4	5
11. the employee benefits provided by the company in addition to pay	1	2	3	4	5
12. being informed of important happenings in the company	1	2	3	4	5
13. the way other departments do their end of the job	1	2	3	4	5
14. the performance of company management in providing leadership	1	2	3	4	5
15. the company procedures for hours and wages	1	2	3	4	5

Please continue on the next page

What do you like about working for this Company?

What changes or suggestions would you recommend to make this a better place to work and a better Company?

Do you have any additional comments you would like to make about—your job—your supervisor—or the Company?

minnesota satisfactoriness scales
1966

Restricted: For Research Use Only

Date sent: _____

Please check the best answer for each question.
Be sure to answer all questions.

Compared to others in his work group, how well does he	not as well	about the same	better
1. follow company policies and practices?	☐	☐	☐
2. accept the direction of his supervisor?	☐	☐	☐
3. follow standard work rules and procedures?	☐	☐	☐
4. perform tasks requiring repetitive movements?	☐	☐	☐
5. accept the responsibility of his job?	☐	☐	☐
6. adapt to changes in procedures or methods?	☐	☐	☐
7. respect the authority of his supervisor?	☐	☐	☐
8. work as a member of a team?	☐	☐	☐
9. get along with his supervisors?	☐	☐	☐
10. perform repetitive tasks?	☐	☐	☐
11. get along with his co-workers?	☐	☐	☐
12. perform tasks requiring variety and change in methods?	☐	☐	☐

Compared to others in his work group	not as good	about the same	better
1. how good is the quality of his work?	☐	☐	☐
2. how good is the quantity of his work?	☐	☐	☐

If you could make the decision, would you	yes	not sure	no
1. give him a pay raise?	☐	☐	☐
2. transfer him to a job at a higher level?	☐	☐	☐
3. promote him to a position of more responsibility?	☐	☐	☐

Compared to others in his work group, how often does he	less	about the same	more
1. come late for work?	☐	☐	☐
2. become overexcited?	☐	☐	☐
3. become upset and unhappy?	☐	☐	☐
4. need disciplinary action?	☐	☐	☐

5. stay absent from work? ☐ ☐ ☐
6. seem bothered by something? ☐ ☐ ☐
7. complain about physical ailments? ☐ ☐ ☐
8. say 'odd' things? ☐ ☐ ☐
9. seem to tire easily? ☐ ☐ ☐
10. act as if he is not listening when spoken to? ☐ ☐ ☐
11. wander from subject to subject when talking? ☐ ☐ ☐

Now will you please consider this worker with respect to his over-all competence, the effectiveness with which he performs his job, his proficiency, his general overall value. Take into account all the elements of successful job performance, such as knowledge of the job and functions performed, quantity and quality of output, relations with other people (subordinates, equals, superiors), ability to get the work done, intelligence, interest, response to training, and the like. In other words, how closely does he approximate the ideal, the kind of worker you want more of? With all these factors in mind, where would you rank this worker as compared with the other people whom you now have doing the same work? (or, if he is the only one, how does he compare with those who have done the same work in the past?)

In the top ¼ ☐
In the top half but not among the top ¼ ☐
In the bottom half but not among the lowest ¼ ☐
In the lowest ¼ ☐

Thank you very much for your cooperation.

minnesota importance questionnaire

1967 Revision

Restricted: For Research Use Only

© Copyright, 1967
Work Adjustment Project
Industrial Relations Center
University of Minnesota

Directions

The purpose of this questionnaire is to find out what you consider **important** in your **ideal job,** the kind of job you would most like to have.

On the following pages you will find **pairs** of statements about work.

    —Read each **pair** of statements carefully.

    —Decide which statement of the **pair** is **more** important to you in your **ideal** job.

    —For each pair mark your choice on the answer sheet. **Do not mark this booklet.** (Directions how to mark the answer sheet are given below.)

Do this for **all** pairs of statements. Work as rapidly as you can. Read each pair of statements, mark your choice, then move on to the next pair. Be sure to make a choice for **every** pair. **Do not** go back to change your answers to any pairs.

Remember: You are to decide which statement of the pair is **more important** to **you** in your **ideal** job. Mark your choice on the answer sheet, **not** on this booklet.

How to Mark the Answer Sheet

First of all

    Print your name in the space provided, and fill in the other information requested.

To fill in the answer sheet

    Start where it is marked "Page 1."

    There is a box for each pair of statements. The number in the middle of the box is the number that pair. "a" and "b" in the box stand for the two statements of the pair.

    If you think statement "a" is more important to you than statement "b", mark an "X" over the "a" on the answer sheet, as shown in the example below:

page	a	a	a
—1—	—2—	—3—
1	b	b	b

However, if you think statement "b" is more important to you than statement "a", mark an "X" over the "b" on the answer sheet, as shown in the example below:

page	a	a	a
—1—	—2—	—3—
1	b	b	b

Mark Only One Answer for Each Pair of Statements.

    Mark **either** "a" **or** "b" for each pair. **Do this for all pairs of statements.** Remember, do not mark your answer on this booklet. Use the answer sheet.

Ask yourself: Which is **more important** to me in my **ideal** job?

1.
a. I could be busy all the time.
        OR
b. The job would provide an opportunity for advancement.

2.
a. I could try out some of my own ideas.
        OR
b. My co-workers would be easy to make friends with.

3.
a. The job could give me a feeling of accomplishment.
        OR
b. I could do something that makes use of my abilities.

4.
a. The company would administer its policies fairly.
        OR
b. I could be busy all the time.

5.
a. I could try out some of my own ideas.
        OR
b. I could be "somebody" in the community.

6.
a. The job would provide an opportunity for advancement.
        OR
b. My co-workers would be easy to make friends with.

7.
a. I could tell people what to do.
        OR
b. I could work alone on the job.

8.
a. I could get recognition for the work I do.
        OR
b. The company would administer its policies fairly.

9.
a. My co-workers would be easy to make friends with.
        OR
b. The job would provide for steady employment.

10.
a. The job could give me a feeling of accomplishment.
        OR
b. The job would provide an opportunity for advancement.

11.
a. My boss would train his men well.
        OR
b. I could work alone on the job.

12.
a. I could do the work without feeling that is is morally wrong.
        OR
b. The job would have good working conditions.

Ask yourself: Which is **more important** to me in my **ideal** job?

a. I could be busy all the time.
13. OR
b. The job could give me a feeling of accomplishment.

a. I could do something that makes use of my abilities.
14. OR
b. The job would provide an opportunity for advancement.

a. I could tell people what to do.
15. OR
b. The company would administer its policies fairly.

a. My co-workers would be easy to make friends with.
16. OR
b. My pay would compare well with that of other workers.

a. I could try out some of my own ideas.
17. OR
b. I could work alone on the job.

a. I could get recognition for the work I do.
18. OR
b. I could do the work without feeling that is is morally wrong.

a. The job would provide for steady employment.
19. OR
b. I could make decisions on my own.

a. I could do things for other people.
20. OR
b. I could be "somebody" in the community.

a. My boss would back up his men (with top management).
21. OR
b. My boss would train his men well.

a. The job would have good working conditions.
22. OR
b. I could do something different every day.

a. I could do something that makes use of my abilities.
23. OR
b. I could be busy all the time.

a. The job could give me a feeling of accomplishment.
24. OR
b. I could tell people what to do.

Ask yourself: Which is *more important* to me in my *ideal* job?

25.
   a. The company would administer its policies fairly.
       OR
   b. The job would provide an opportunity for advancement.

26.
   a. I could do something that makes use of my abilities.
       OR
   b. My co-workers would be easy to make friends with.

27.
   a. I could try out some of my own ideas.
       OR
   b. The job could give me a feeling of accomplishment.

28.
   a. I could be busy all the time.
       OR
   b. I could work alone on the job.

29.
   a. The job would provide an opportunity for advancement.
       OR
   b. I could do the work without feeling that it is morally wrong.

30.
   a. I could tell people what to do.
       OR
   b. I could get recognition for the work I do.

31.
   a. The company would administer its policies fairly.
       OR
   b. I could make decisions on my own.

32.
   a. The job would provide for steady employment.
       OR
   b. My pay would compare well with that of other workers.

33.
   a. I could do things for other people.
       OR
   b. My co-workers would be easy to make friends with.

34.
   a. My boss would back up his men (with top management).
       OR
   b. I could work alone on the job.

35.
   a. I could do the work without feeling that it is morally wrong.
       OR
   b. My boss would train his men well.

36.
   a. I could do something different every day.
       OR
   b. I could get recognition for the work I do.

Ask yourself: Which is **more important** to me in my **ideal** job?

37.
a. I could make decisions on my own.
    OR
b. The job would have good working conditions.

38.
a. I could do something that makes use of my abilities.
    OR
b. I could tell people what to do.

39.
a. The company would administer its policies fairly.
    OR
b. The job could give me a feeling of accomplishment.

40.
a. I could be busy all the time.
    OR
b. My pay would compare well with that of other workers.

41.
a. I could try out some of my own ideas.
    OR
b. I could tell people what to do.

42.
a. I could get recognition for the work I do.
    OR
b. My co-workers would be easy to make friends with.

43.
a. The company would administer its policies fairly.
    OR
b. I could work alone on the job.

44.
a. I could do the work without feeling that is is morally wrong.
    OR
b. My pay would compare well with that of other workers.

45.
a. I could make decisions on my own.
    OR
b. I could try out some of my own ideas.

46.
a. The job would provide for steady employment.
    OR
b. I could work alone on the job.

47.
a. I could do things for other people.
    OR
b. I could do the work without feeling that it is morally wrong.

48.
a. I could get recognition for the work I do.
    OR
b. I could be "somebody" in the community.

Ask yourself: Which is **more important** to me in my **ideal** job?

49.
a. I could make decisions on my own.
   OR
b. My boss would back up his men (with top management).

50.
a. The job would provide for steady employment.
   OR
b. My boss would train his men well.

51.
a. I could do something different every day.
   OR
b. I could do things for other people.

52.
a. The job would have good working conditions.
   OR
b. I could be "somebody" in the community.

53.
a. I could tell people what to do.
   OR
b. I could be busy all the time.

54.
a. The job would provide an opportunity for advancement.
   OR
b. My pay would compare well with that of other workers.

55.
a. I could do something that makes use of my abilities.
   OR
b. The company would administer its policies fairly.

56.
a. I could be busy all the time.
   OR
b. My co-workers would be easy to make friends with.

57.
a. The job could give me a feeling of accomplishment.
   OR
b. My pay would compare well with that of other workers.

58.
a. I could try out some of my own ideas.
   OR
b. The job would provide an opportunity for advancement.

59.
a. The company would administer its policies fairly.
   OR
b. I could do the work without feeling that it is morally wrong.

60.
a. I could get recognition for the work I do.
   OR
b. My pay would compare well with that of other workers.

Ask yourself: Which is **more important** to me in my **ideal** job?

a. My co-workers would be easy to make friends with.
61.   OR
b. I could make decisions on my own.

a. The job would provide for steady employment.
62.   OR
b. I could try out some of my own ideas.

a. I could work alone on the job.
63.   OR
b. I could do things for other people.

a. I could be "somebody" in the community.
64.   OR
b. I could do the work without feeling that is is morally wrong.

a. The job would provide an opportunity for advancement.
65.   OR
b. I could tell people what to do.

a. My boss would train his men well.
66.   OR
b. I could make decisions on my own.

a. The job would provide for steady employment.
67.   OR
b. I could do something different every day.

a. I could do things for other people.
68.   OR
b. The job would have good working conditions.

a. My boss would back up his men (with top management).
69.   OR
b. I could get recognition for the work I do.

a. My co-workers would be easy to make friends with.
70.   OR
b. I could tell people what to do.

a. The company would administer its policies fairly.
71.   OR
b. I could try out some of my own ideas.

a. My pay would compare well with that of other workers.
72.   OR
b. I could work alone on the job.

Ask yourself: Which is **more important** to me in my **ideal** job?

73.
a. I could do the work without feeling that it is morally wrong.
    OR
b. My co-workers would be easy to make friends with.

74.
a. My boss would back up his men (with top management).
    OR
b. The job would have good working conditions.

75.
a. I could work alone on the job.
    OR
b. I could make my decisions on my own.

76.
a. The job would provide for steady employment.
    OR
b. I could do the work without feeling that it is morally wrong.

77.
a. I could get recognition for the work I do.
    OR
b. I could do things for other people.

78.
a. I could be "somebody" in the community.
    OR
b. I could make decisions on my own.

79.
a. My boss would back up his men (with top management).
    OR
b. The job would provide for steady employment.

80.
a. My boss would train his men well.
    OR
b. I could do things for other people.

81.
a. I could do something different every day.
    OR
b. I could be "somebody" in the community.

82.
a. I could get recognition for the work I do.
    OR
b. I could try out some of my own ideas.

83.
a. My pay would compare well with that of other workers.
    OR
b. I could tell people what to do.

84.
a. I could do something that makes use of my abilities.
    OR
b. The job would have good working conditions.

Ask yourself: Which is **more important** to me in my **ideal** job?

a. I could do something different every day.
85.   OR
b. The job could give me a feeling of accomplishment.

a. My boss would train his men well.
86.   OR
b. I could be busy all the time.

a. My co-workers would be easy to make friends with.
87.   OR
b. The company would administer its policies fairly.

a. My pay would compare well with that of other workers.
88.   OR
b. I could try out some of my own ideas.

a. I could do something that makes use of my abilities.
89.   OR
b. I could do something different every day.

a. The job could give me a feeling of accomplishment.
90.   OR
b. The job would have good working conditions.

a. I could work alone on the job.
91.   OR
b. My co-workers would be easy to make friends with.

a. I could do the work without feeling that it is morally wrong.
92.   OR
b. I could try out some of my own ideas.

a. I could get recognition for the work I do.
93.   OR
b. The job would provide for steady employment.

a. My boss would train his men well.
94.   OR
b. I could do something that makes use of my abilities.

a. I could be busy all the time.
95.   OR
b. The job would have good working conditions.

a. I could do things for other people.
96.   OR
b. I could make decisions on my own.

Ask yourself: Which is **more important** to me in my **ideal** job?

97.
   a. The job would provide for steady employment.
       OR
   b. I could be "somebody" in the community.

98.
   a. I could work alone on the job.
       OR
   b. I could get recognition for the work I do.

99.
   a. I could do things for other people.
       OR
   b. My boss would back up his men (with top management).

100.
   a. I could make decisions on my own.
       OR
   b. I could do the work without feeling that it is morally wrong.

101.
   a. My boss would train his men well.
       OR
   b. I could be "somebody" in the community.

102.
   a. My boss would back up his men (with top management).
       OR
   b. I could do something different every day.

103.
   a. I could get recognition for the work I do.
       OR
   b. I could make decisions on my own.

104.
   a. I could be busy all the time.
       OR
   b. I could do something different every day.

105.
   a. My boss would train his men well.
       OR
   b. The job could give me a feeling of accomplishment.

106.
   a. The job would have good working conditions.
       OR
   b. The job would provide an opportunity for advancement.

107.
   a. My pay would compare well with that of other workers.
       OR
   b. The company would administer its policies fairly.

108.
   a. I could do the work without feeling that it is morally wrong.
       OR
   b. I could work alone on the job.

Ask yourself: Which is **more important** to me in my **ideal** job?

a. My boss would train his men well.
109.   OR
b. The job would have good working conditions.

a. My boss would back up his men (with top management).
110.   OR
b. I could do something that makes use of my abilities.

a. The job would provide for steady employment.
111.   OR
b. I could do things for other people.

a. The job could give me a feeling of accomplishment.
112.   OR
b. My co-workers would be easy to make friends with.

a. I could do something different every day.
113.   OR
b. My boss would train his men well.

a. I could do things for other people.
114.   OR
b. I could try out some of my own ideas.

a. I could do something that makes use of my abilities.
115.   OR
b. I could be "somebody" in the community.

a. My boss would back up his men (with top management).
116.   OR
b. The job could give me a feeling of accomplishment.

a. The job would provide an opportunity for advancement.
117.   OR
b. I could do something different every day.

a. I could tell people what to do.
118.   OR
b. The job would have good working conditions.

a. I could do the work without feeling that it is morally wrong.
119.   OR
b. My boss would back up his men (with top management).

a. My pay would compare well with that of other workers.
120.   OR
b. I could make decisions on my own.

Ask yourself: Which is **more important** to me in my **ideal** job?

a. I could be "somebody" in the community.
121.   OR
b. I could work alone on the job.

a. My boss would train his men well.
122.   OR
b. I could get recognition for the work I do.

a. I could make decisions on my own.
123.   OR
b. I could do something different every day.

a. The job would have good working conditions.
124.   OR
b. The job would provide for steady employment.

a. My pay would compare well with that of other workers.
125.   OR
b. I could do something that makes use of my abilities.

a. I could do something different every day.
126.   OR
b. I could tell people what to do.

a. My boss would back up his men (with top management).
127.   OR
b. I could be "somebody" in the community.

a. I could try out some of my own ideas.
128.   OR
b. I could be busy all the time.

a. I could work alone on the job.
129.   OR
b. The job would provide an opportunity for advancement.

a. I could tell people what to do.
130.   OR
b. I could do the work without feeling that it is morally wrong.

a. The job would have good working conditions.
131.   OR
b. The company would administer its policies fairly.

a. My boss would train his men well.
132.   OR
b. The job would provide an opportunity for advancement.

Ask yourself: Which is **more important** to me in my **ideal** job?

133.
a. My boss would back up his men (with top management).
    OR
b. I could be busy all the time.

134.
a. The job could give me a feeling of accomplishment.
    OR
b. I could be "somebody" in the community.

135.
a. I could do something that makes use of my abilities.
    OR
b. I could do things for other people.

136.
a. I could do the work without feeling that it is morally wrong.
    OR
b. I could do something different every day.

137.
a. The job would have good working conditions.
    OR
b. I could get recognition for the work I do.

138.
a. My pay would compare well with that of other workers.
    OR
b. I could do things for other people.

139.
a. I could be "somebody" in the community.
    OR
b. My co-workers would be easy to make friends with.

140.
a. I could try out some of my own ideas.
    OR
b. My boss would back up his men (with top management).

141.
a. The job could give me a feeling of accomplishment.
    OR
b. I could work alone on the job.

142.
a. I could do the work without feeling that it is morally wrong.
    OR
b. I could be busy all the time.

143.
a. The job would provide an opportunity for advancement.
    OR
b. I could get recognition for the work I do.

144.
a. I could tell people what to do.
    OR
b. I could make decisions on my own.

Ask yourself: Which is **more important** to me in my **ideal** job?

145.
a. The company would administer its policies fairly.
    OR
b. The job would provide for steady employment.

146.
a. I could try out some of my own ideas.
    OR
b. I could do something that makes use of my abilities.

147.
a. My pay would compare well with that of other workers.
    OR
b. The job would have good working conditions.

148.
a. I could do something different every day.
    OR
b. The company would administer its policies fairly.

149.
a. My boss would train his men well.
    OR
b. I could tell people what to do.

150.
a. My boss would back up his men (with top management).
    OR
b. The job would provide an opportunity for advancement.

151.
a. I could be busy all the time.
    OR
b. I could be "somebody" in the community.

152.
a. I could do things for other people.
    OR
b. The job could give me a feeling of accomplishment.

153.
a. I could do something that makes use of my abilities.
    OR
b. The job would provide for steady employment.

154.
a. I could do something different every day.
    OR
b. I could work alone on the job.

155.
a. I could try out some of my own ideas.
    OR
b. My boss would train his men well.

156.
a. My co-workers would be easy to make friends with.
    OR
b. My boss would back up his men (with top management).

Ask yourself: Which is **more important** to me in my **ideal** job?

a. I could be "somebody" in the community.
157.   OR
b. My pay would compare well with that of other workers.

a. I could do things for other people.
158.   OR
b. The company would administer its policies fairly.

a. The job would provide for steady employment.
159.   OR
b. I could tell people what to do.

a. The job would provide an opportunity for advancement.
160.   OR
b. I could make decisions on my own.

a. I could be busy all the time.
161.   OR
b. I could get recognition for the work I do.

a. I could do the work without feeling that it is morally wrong.
162.   OR
b. The job could give me a feeling of accomplishment.

a. I could work alone on the job.
163.   OR
b. I could do something that makes use of my abilities.

a. The job would have good working conditions.
164.   OR
b. My co-workers would be easy to make friends with.

a. I could do something different every day.
165.   OR
b. My pay would compare well with that of other workers.

a. My boss would train his men well.
166.   OR
b. The company would administer its policies fairly.

a. I could tell people what to do.
167.   OR
b. My boss would back up his men (with top management).

a. The job would provide an opportunity for advancement.
168.   OR
b. I could be "somebody" in the community.

Ask yourself: Which is **more important** to me in my *ideal* job?

169.
a. I could do things for other people.
    OR
b. I could be busy all the time.

170.
a. The job could give me a feeling of accomplishment.
    OR
b. The job would provide for steady employment.

171.
a. I could make decisions on my own.
    OR
b. I could do something that makes use of my abilities.

172.
a. I could work alone on the job.
    OR
b. The job would have good working conditions.

173.
a. I could do something different every day.
    OR
b. I could try out some of my own ideas.

174.
a. My co-workers would be easy to make friends with.
    OR
b. My boss would train his men well.

175.
a. My boss would back up his men (with top management).
    OR
b. My pay would compare well with that of other workers.

176.
a. I could be "somebody" in the community.
    OR
b. The company would administer its policies fairly.

177.
a. I could tell people what to do.
    OR
b. I could do things for other people.

178.
a. The job would provide an opportunity for advancement.
    OR
b. The job would provide for steady employment.

179.
a. I could be busy all the time.
    OR
b. I could make decisions on my own.

180.
a. I could get recognition for the work I do.
    OR
b. The job could give me a feeling of accomplishment.

Ask yourself: Which is **more important** to me in my **ideal** job?

181.
a. I could do something that makes use of my abilities.
OR
b. I could do the work without feeling that it is morally wrong.

182.
a. The job would have good working conditions.
OR
b. I could try out some of my own ideas.

183.
a. My co-workers would be easy to make friends with.
OR
b. I could do something different every day.

184.
a. My boss would train his men well.
OR
b. My pay would compare well with that of other workers.

185.
a. The company would administer its policies fairly.
OR
b. My boss would back up his men (with top management).

186.
a. I could tell people what to do.
OR
b. I could be "somebody" in the community.

187.
a. The job would provide an opportunity for advancement.
OR
b. I could do things for other people.

188.
a. I could be busy all the time.
OR
b. The job would provide for steady employment.

189.
a. I could make decisions on my own.
OR
b. The job could give me a feeling of accomplishment.

190.
a. I could get recognition for the work I do.
OR
b. I could do something that makes use of my abilities.

Please continue on the next page.

this page consider each statement and decide whether or not it is *important* to have in your *ideal job.*

—If you think that the statement is *important* for your *ideal job,* mark an X in the **"Yes"** box on your answer sheet.

—If you think that the statement is *not important* for your *ideal job,* mark an X in the **"No"** box on your answer sheet.

On my *ideal job* it is important that . . .

191. I could do something that makes use of my abilities.

192. the job could give me a feeling of accomplishment.

193. I could be busy all the time.

194. the job would provide an opportunity for advancement.

195. I could tell people what to do.

196. the company would administer its policies fairly.

197. my pay would compare well with that of other workers.

198. my co-workers would be easy to make friends with.

199. I could try out some of my own ideas.

200. I could work alone on the job.

201. I could do the work without feeling that it is morally wrong.

202. I could get recognition for the work I do.

203. I could make decisions on my own.

204. the job would provide for steady employment.

205. I could do things for other people.

206. I could be "somebody" in the community.

207. my boss would back up his men (with top management).

208. my boss would train his men well.

209. I could do something different every day.

210. the job would have good working conditions.

Please check your answer sheet to see that you have marked only one choice in each of the 210 boxes.

a sample occupational reinforcer pattern

Counselor, Vocational Rehabilitation
(N = 46 Supervisors)

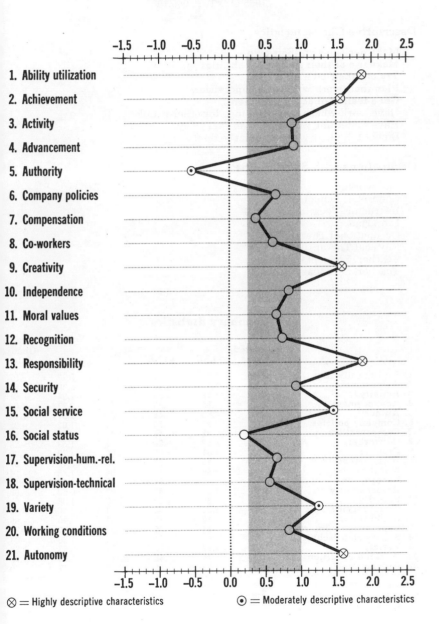

⊗ = Highly descriptive characteristics   ⊙ = Moderately descriptive characteristics

Counselor, Vocational Rehabilitation

(N = 46 Supervisors)

1965 D.O.T. = 045.108

Descriptive Characteristics

Make decisions on their own
Make use of their individual abilities
Try out their own ideas
Plan their work with little supervision
Get a feeling of accomplishment
Have work where they do things for other people
Have something different to do every day
Do not tell other workers what to do

Occupations with Similar ORPs

Caseworker
Counselor, School
Instructor, Vocational School
Librarian
Occupational Therapist
Physical Therapist
Teacher, Elementary School
Teacher, Secondary School

Summary Statistics

	Adjusted Value	−1 SE	+1 SE	P	Q	Unadj. Value
1. Ability utilization	1.85	1.78	1.94	0.00	5.72	.97
2. Achievement	1.56	1.51	1.62	.02	5.30	.68
3. Activity	.87	.78	.95	.15	1.94	−.01
4. Advancement	.90	.85	.95	.02	2.77	.02
5. Authority	−.55	−.63	−.48	.89	1.37	−1.43
6. Company policies	.63	.57	.70	.17	1.62	−.25
7. Compensation	.36	.28	.45	.43	.78	−.51
8. Co-workers	.60	.53	.66	.07	1.53	−.28
9. Creativity	1.58	1.51	1.65	0.00	4.79	.70
10. Independence	.81	.70	.93	.33	1.40	−.07
11. Moral values	.64	.56	.73	.04	1.38	−.24
12. Recognition	.73	.65	.81	.33	1.68	−.15
13. Responsibility	1.86	1.80	1.92	.02	6.62	.98
14. Security	.91	.82	1.00	0.00	1.98	.03
15. Social service	1.47	1.38	1.56	.04	3.56	.59
16. Social status	.19	.10	.27	.54	.40	−.69
17. Supervision-hum.-rel.	.64	.58	.70	.09	1.77	−.24
18. Supervision-technical	.54	.46	.61	.28	1.28	−.34
19. Variety	1.26	1.19	1.32	.07	3.63	.38
20. Working conditions	.81	.74	.89	.17	1.94	−.06
21. Autonomy	1.58	1.50	1.65	0.00	4.57	.70
Adjusted neutral point	0.000	−.051	.049			
Unadjusted neutral point	−.879	−.930	−.830			

Confidential
For Research
Purposes Only

job description questionnaire

On the following pages you are asked to rank statements
on the basis of how well they describe the job of:

_____

Statements about this job are in groups of five. You are asked to consider *each group* of five *individually* and rank the five statements in terms
of *how well they describe the job*, using the numbers "1" to "5." Then go
to the next group of five statements and make the same kind of ranking.

For example, your answers on a group of statements might look like
this:

Workers on this job . . .

4	get full credit for the work they do.
3	are of service to other people.
1	have freedom to use their own judgment.
5	do new and original things on their own.
2	have the chance to get ahead.

This means that, of the five statements, you consider "have freedom to
use their own judgment" as most descriptive of the job; "have the
chance to get ahead" as the next most descriptive statement; and so on.

You will find some of these comparisons more difficult to make than
others, but it is *important* that you rank *every statement* in each group.

All information will be held in strictest confidence.

work adjustment project

industrial relations center

university of minnesota

© Copyright 1967
All rights reserved

Please rank the five statements in each group on the basis of how well they describe the job mentioned on the front page. Write a "1" by the statement which best describes the job; write a "2" by the statement which provides the next best description; continue ranking all five statements, using a "5" for the statement which describes the job least well.

Workers on this job . . .

_____are busy all the time.

_____have work where they do things for other people.

_____try out their own ideas.

_____are paid well in comparison with other workers.

_____have opportunities for advancement.

Workers on this job . . .

_____have work where they do things for other people.

_____have something different to do every day.

_____get a feeling of accomplishment.

_____have bosses who train their men well.

_____have a company which administers its policies fairly.

Workers on this job . . .

_____do work without feeling that it is morally wrong.

_____have bosses who back up their men (with top management).

_____have something different to do every day.

_____make use of their individual abilities.

_____are busy all the time.

Workers on this job . . .

_____have a company which administers its policies fairly.

_____try out their own ideas.

_____make use of their individual abilities.

_____have co-workers who are easy to make friends with.

_____have the position of "somebody" in the community.

Please rank the five statements in each *group on the basis of* how well *they* describe *the job mentioned on the front page. Write a "1" by the statement which* best *describes the job; write a "2" by the statement which provides the* next best *description; continue ranking all five statements, using a "5" for the statement which describes the job* least *well.*

Workers on this job . . .

_____ do their work alone.

_____ have the position of "somebody" in the community.

_____ have work where they do things for other people.

_____ have bosses who back up their men (with top management).

_____ make decisions on their own.

Workers on this job . . .

_____ try out their own ideas.

_____ receive recognition for the work they do.

_____ have something different to do every day.

_____ do their work alone.

_____ have steady employment.

Workers on this job . . .

_____ have opportunities for advancement.

_____ make use of their individual abilities.

_____ receive recognition for the work they do.

_____ make decisions on their own.

_____ have bosses who train their men well.

Workers on this job . . .

_____ have good working conditions.

_____ do their work alone.

_____ have a company which administers its policies fairly.

_____ have opportunities for advancement.

_____ do work without feeling that it is morally wrong.

Please rank the five statements in each group on the basis of how well they describe the job mentioned on the front page. Write a "1" by the statement which best describes the job; write a "2" by the statement which provides the next best description; continue ranking all five statements, using a "5" for the statement which describes the job least well.

Workers on this job . . .

_____make use of their individual abilities.

_____tell other workers what to do.

_____have good working conditions.

_____have steady employment.

_____have work where they do things for other people.

Workers on this job . . .

_____make decisions on their own.

_____are busy all the time.

_____have steady employment.

_____have a company which administers its policies fairly.

_____plan their work with little supervision.

Workers on this job . . .

_____get a feeling of accomplishment.

_____make decisions on their own.

_____tell other workers what to do.

_____do work without feeling that it is morally wrong.

_____try out their own ideas.

Workers on this job . . .

_____have co-workers who are easy to make friends with.

_____have steady employment.

_____have opportunities for advancement.

_____have bosses who back up their men (with top management).

_____get a feeling of accomplishment.

Please rank the five statements in each group on the basis of how well they describe the job mentioned on the front page. Write a "1" by the statement which best describes the job; write a "2" by the statement which provides the next best description; continue ranking all five statements, using a "5" for the statement which describes the job least well.

Workers on this job . . .

_____plan their work with little supervision.

_____have opportunities for advancement.

_____have the position of "somebody" in the community.

_____tell other workers what to do.

_____have something different to do every day.

Workers on this job . . .

_____are paid well in comparison with other workers.

_____get a feeling of accomplishment.

_____do their work alone.

_____plan their work with little supervision.

_____make use of their individual abilities.

Workers on this job . . .

_____tell other workers what to do.

_____have bosses who train their men well.

_____have co-workers who are easy to make friends with.

_____are busy all the time.

_____do their work alone.

Workers on this job . . .

_____have steady employment.

_____are paid well in comparison with other workers.

_____have bosses who train their men well.

_____have the position of "somebody" in the community.

_____do work without feeling that it is morally wrong.

please continue on the next page

Please rank the five statements in each group on the basis of how well they describe the job mentioned on the front page. Write a "1" by the statement which best describes the job; write a "2" by the statement which provides the next best description; continue ranking all five statements, using a "5" for the statement which describes the job least well.

Workers on this job . . .

_____have bosses who train their men well.

_____plan their work with little supervision.

_____have bosses who back up their men (with top management).

_____try out their own ideas.

_____have good working conditions.

Workers on this job . . .

_____receive recognition for the work they do.

_____do work without feeling that it is morally wrong.

_____plan their work with little supervision.

_____have work where they do things for other people.

_____have co-workers who are easy to make friends with.

Workers on this job . . .

_____have bosses who back up their men (with top management).

_____have a company which administers its policies fairly.

_____are paid well in comparison with other workers.

_____receive recognition for the work they do.

_____tell other workers what to do.

Workers on this job . . .

_____have something different to do every day.

_____have co-workers who are easy to make friends with.

_____make decisions on their own.

_____have good working conditions.

_____are paid well in comparison with other workers.

please continue on the next page

Please rank these five statements.

Workers on this job . . .

_____have the position of "somebody" in the community.

_____have good working conditions.

_____are busy all the time.

_____get a feeling of accomplishment.

_____receive recognition for the work they do.

===

On the rest of this page we are asking you to do something different. *This time, consider each statement* individually *and decide* whether or not it *describes the job.*

—If you think that the statement describes the job, circle "Yes."

—If you think that the statement does not describe the job, circle "No."

	Circle your answer	
Workers on this job . . .	for each statement	
1. make use of their individual abilities	Yes	No
2. get a feeling of accomplishment	Yes	No
3. are busy all the time	Yes	No
4. have opportunities for advancement	Yes	No
5. tell other workers what to do	Yes	No
6. have a company which administers its policies fairly	Yes	No
7. are paid well in comparison with other workers	Yes	No
8. have co-workers who are easy to make friends with	Yes	No
9. try out their own ideas	Yes	No
10. do their work alone	Yes	No
11. do work without feeling that it is morally wrong	Yes	No
12. receive recognition for the work they do	Yes	No
13. make decisions on their own	Yes	No
14. have steady employment	Yes	No
15. have work where they do things for other people	Yes	No
16. have the position of "somebody" in the community	Yes	No
17. have bosses who back up their men (with top management)	Yes	No
18. have bosses who train their men well	Yes	No
19. have something different to do every day	Yes	No
20. have good working conditions	Yes	No
21. plan their work with little supervision	Yes	No

please continue on the next page

Please answer these questions as a supervisor of people working on the job of_____.

1. How long have you been a supervisor of people working on this job?
   _____years   _____months

2. How many workers do you usually supervise on this job? (not including yourself)?_____
   How many are men?_____   How many are women?_____

3. Have you ever been a worker on this job? (check one)
   ☐ No
   ☐ Yes—how long did you work on this job?
     _____years   _____months
   Are you now a worker on this job, in addition to being a supervisor? (check one)
   ☐ Yes   ☐ No

4. Compared with other supervisors of people working on this job, how well would you say you are acquainted with this job? (check one)
   ☐ Not as well acquainted as most supervisors on this job
   ☐ About as well acquainted as most supervisors on this job
   ☐ Better acquainted than most supervisors on this job

5. Please answer the following questions about yourself.
   Sex: ☐ Male ☐ Female   Age_____
   Circle the number of years of schooling completed in each category.

Grade and High School	Business or Trade School	College (including graduate and professional school)
7 8 9 10 11 12	0 1 2 3 4 5	0 1 2 3 4 5 6 7

   Your job title_____

6. How long have you been with your present organization? _____years

7. On the preceding pages you answered questions about statements describing this job. Please list below any other characteristics which you think are important for describing this job.

   _____

   _____

   _____

Thank you very much for your assistance.

Glossary
References
Index

Glossary

Ability dimensions. Basic dimensions, representing common elements in skill dimensions, used to describe individual behavior in parsimonious terms.

Ability requirements. Minimum levels of several abilities required of a worker to predict satisfactoriness.

Correspondence. A relationship in which an individual and his environment are mutually responsive.

Correspondence, in work setting. A relationship in which an individual fulfills the requirements of the work environment, and the work environment fulfills the requirements of the individual.

Interests. Preferences for activities, deriving from the interaction of an individual's needs and abilities.

Interests, exhibited. Preferences for activities, inferred from observation of an individual's participation in activities or from records of such participation.

Interests, expressed or stated. Preferences for activities as stated by an individual.

Interests, measured. Preferences for activities as indicated by an individual on a structured standardized psychometric instrument designed to sample a broad range of classes of activity preferences.

Interests, validated. Preferences for activities, based on agreement between measured and exhibited interests for an individual.

Need dimensions. Basic dimensions, representing common elements in reinforcement-value dimensions, used to describe in parsimonious terms an individual's experience with or evaluation of stimulus conditions.

Personality. The unique pattern of stable characteristics that distinguishes a responding organism as an individual.

Personality description, exhibited. The description of an individual's personality, based on observation of his behavior or on records of his behavior.

Personality description, expressed or stated. The description of an individual's personality in terms of the likelihood of his behaving in particular ways under given conditions.

Personality description, measured. The description of an individual's personality within the framework of a structured standardized psychometric instrument designed to sample a broad range of classes of alternative behaviors under given conditions.

Personality description, validated. The description of an individual's personality, based on the agreement between measured and exhibited personality descriptions.

Personality structure.   The abilities, needs, and interaction of abilities and needs, of an individual.

Personality style.   An individual's characteristic manner of utilizing his abilities (style of responding) and satisfying his needs (style of reacting to stimulus conditions).

Preferences.   An individual's description of his norms for stimulus conditions or activities. These norms are derived from his experience with stimulus conditions or activities and his evaluation of how satisfying the experiences were.

Psychological needs.   The reinforcement values of stimulus conditions. This differs from common usage in which the term *need* is used to denote a state of deprivation.

Reinforcement.   The maintenance or increase of responding associated with either the presence of or the introduction of reinforcers.

Reinforcement values.   The degree to which stimulus conditions function as reinforcers for an individual. Reinforcement values may be actual (experienced by the individual), stated (reported by the individual), or observed (reported by an observer).

Reinforcement-value dimension.   A dimension along which different reinforcement values are observed for different individuals but for the same stimulus condition.

Reinforcer system.   The need-satisfying characteristics of the work environment. This system can be described in terms of the minimum levels of reinforcement values for several reinforcers required to predict the satisfaction of an individual.

Reinforcers.   Stimulus conditions consistently associated with the maintenance or increase of responding.

Satisfaction.   Fullfillment of the requirements of an individual by the work environment.

Satisfactoriness.   Fulfillment of the requirements of the work environment by an individual.

Skill dimension.   A skill observed to be common for several individuals who differ in degrees of skillfulness.

Skillfulness.   A ranking of different individuals along a skill dimension in terms of such characteristics as level of skill-difficulty attained, economy of effort, and efficiency of behavior.

Skills.   Recurring response sequences in the observed behavior of an individual.

Stability.   Relatively little change in repeated measurements of an individual's personality characteristics (his abilities and needs).

Tenure.   Remaining in a job as a manifestation of correspondence between an individual and his work environment.

Work adjustment.   The continuous and dynamic process by which the individual seeks to achieve and maintain correspondence with his work environment.

Work environment.   The setting in which work behavior takes place, described in terms of ability requirements and need-satisfying characteristics.

Work personality.   The abilities and needs of an individual that are most relevant to work behavior, and the characteristic functioning of these abilities and needs in the work setting.

References

Anastasi, A. *Differential psychology.* (3rd ed.) New York: Macmillan, 1958.

Bakke, E. W. *The unemployed man.* New York: Dutton, 1934.

Bakke, E. W. *The unemployed worker.* New Haven: Yale University Press, 1940.

Bennett, G. K., Seashore, H. G., & Wesman, A. G. *Differential Aptitude Tests.* New York: Psychological Corporation, 1947-1959.

Borgen, F. H., Weiss, D. J., Tinsley, H. E. A., Dawis, R. V., & Lofquist, L. H. Occupational Reinforcer Patterns. *Minnesota Studies in Vocational Rehabilitation,* XXIV, 1968.

Brayfield, A. H. Vocational counseling today. In Williamson, E. G. (Ed.), *Vocational counseling, a reappraisal in honor of Donald G. Paterson.* Minneapolis: University of Minnesota Press, 1961.

Brayfield, A. H., & Rothe, H. F. An index of job satisfaction. *Journal of Applied Psychology,* 1951, *35,* 307-311.

Campbell, D. P. *Manual for Strong Vocational Interest Blanks, Revised.* Stanford, California: Stanford University Press, 1966.

Carlson, R. E. A test of selected hypotheses from the Theory of Work Adjustment. Unpublished doctoral dissertation, University of Minnesota, 1965.

Carlson, R. E., Dawis, R. V., England, G. W., & Lofquist, L. H. The measurement of employment satisfaction. *Minnesota Studies in Vocational Rehabilitation,* XIII, 1962.

Carlson, R. E., Dawis, R. V., England, G. W., and Lofquist, L. H. The measurement of employment satisfactoriness. *Minnesota Studies in Vocational Rehabilitation,* XIV, 1963.

Centers, R. *The psychology of social classes, a study of class consciousness.* Princeton: Princeton University Press, 1949.

Clark, K. E. *The vocational interests of non-professional men.* Minneapolis: University of Minnesota Press, 1961.

Darley, J. G., and Hagenah, T. *Vocational interest measurement.* Minneapolis: University of Minnesota Press, 1955.

Dawis, R. V., England, G. W., & Lofquist, L. H. A theory of work adjustment. *Minnesota Studies in Vocational Rehabilitation,* XV, 1964.

Dawis, R. V., Lofquist, L. H., & Weiss, D. J. A theory of work adjustment (a revision). *Minnesota Studies in Vocational Rehabilitation,* XXIII, 1968.

Dawis, R. V., Weiss, D. J., Lofquist, L. H., & Betz, E. Satisfaction as a moderator in the prediction of satisfactoriness. *Proceedings, 75th Annual Convention, American Psychological Association,* 1967, 269-270.

Deeg, M. E., & Paterson, D. G. Changes in social status of occupations. *Occupations,* 1947, *25,* 205-208.

Dunnette, M. D. *Personnel selection and placement.* Belmont, California: Wadsworth, 1966.

Dvorak, B. J. Differential occupational ability patterns. *Bulletin of the Employment Stabilization Research Institute,* Vol. III, No. 3, February, 1935.

Dvorak, B. J. The general aptitude test battery. *Personnel and Guidance Journal,* 1956, *35,* 145-154.

Dvorak, B. J. The general aptitude test battery. In Super, D. E. (Ed.), *The use of multifactor tests in guidance.* Washington: American Personnel and Guidance Association, 1958.

England, G. W. *Development and use of weighted application blanks.* Dubuque: Brown, 1961.

French, J. W. *Manual for kit of selected tests for reference aptitude and achievement factors.* Princeton: Educational Testing Service, 1954.

Friedman, E. A., & Havighurst, R. *The meaning of work and retirement.* Chicago: University of Chicago Press, 1954.

Garrett, H. E. A developmental theory of intelligence. *American Psychologist,* 1946, *1,* 372-378.

Garrett, J. F., & Levine, E. S. *Psychological practices with the physically disabled.* New York: Columbia University Press, 1962.

Ghiselli, E. E. *The validity of occupational aptitude tests.* New York: Wiley, 1966.

Gilbert, W. M., & Ewing, T. N. Counseling by teaching machine procedures. Paper read at the 1964 meetings of the American Psychological Association.

Gross, M. L. *The brain watchers.* New York: Random House, Inc., 1962.

Guion, R. M. *Personnel testing.* New York: McGraw, 1965.

Hardin, E. *Measurement of physical output at the job level.* Research and Technical Report 10, Industrial Relations Center, University of Minnesota, 1951.

Harman, H. H. *Modern factor analysis.* Chicago: University of Chicago Press, 1960.

Heron, A. A. A psychological study of occupational adjustment. *Journal of Applied Psychology*, 1952, *36*, 385-387.

Hewer, V. H., & Neubeck, G. Occupations of fathers and mothers of entering University of Minnesota freshmen, fall, 1959. *Personnel and Guidance Journal*, 1962, *40*, 622-627.

Hooker, D. Early fetal activities in mammals. *Yale Journal of Biology and Medicine*, 1936, *8*, 579-602.

Hoppock, R. *Job satisfaction.* New York: Harper, 1935.

Hoyt, K. B., & Loughary, J. W. Aquaintance with, and use of referral sources by Iowa secondary school counselors. *Personnel and Guidance Journal*, 1958, *36*, 388-391.

Kerr, W. A. On the validity and reliability of the job satisfaction tear ballot. *Journal of Applied Psychology*, 1948, *32*, 275-281.

Kuder, G. F. *Kuder Preference Record—Occupational.* Chicago: Science Research Associates, 1958.

Kuder, G. F. *Kuder Preference Record—Vocational.* Chicago: Science Research Associates, 1956.

Locke, E. A., Smith, P. C., Kendall, L. M., Hulin, C. L., & Miller, A. Convergent and discriminant validity for areas and methods of rating job satisfaction. *Journal of Applied Psychology*, 1964, *48*, 313-319.

Lofquist, L. H., Siess, T. F., Dawis, R. V., England, G. W., & Weiss, D. J. Disability and work. *Minnesota Studies in Vocational Rehabilitation*, XVII, 1964.

McGowan, J. F. (Ed.) *Counselor development in American society.* Conference recommendations from invitational conference on government-university relations in the professional preparation and employment of counselors, 1965.

Münsterberg, H. *Psychology and industrial efficiency.* Cambridge: Harvard University Press, 1924.

National Council on Rehabilitation. *Symposium report.* New York: National Council on Rehabilitation, 1942.

Osgood, C. E., & Stagner, R. Analysis of a prestige frame of reference by a gradient technique. *Journal of Applied Psychology*, 1941, *25*, 275-290.

Parnes, H. S. *Research on labor mobility.* New York: Social Science Research Council, 1954.

Parsons, F. *Choosing a vocation.* Boston: Houghton, 1909.

Paterson, D. G., Gerken, C. d'A., & Hahn, M. E. *The Minnesota occupational rating scales.* Chicago: Science Research Associates, 1941.

Paterson, D. G., Gerken, C. d'A., & Hahn, M. E. *Revised Minnesota*

182   **References**

occupational rating scales. Minneapolis: University of Minnesota Press, 1953.

Pieper, J. *Leisure, the basis of culture.* New York: Pantheon Books, 1952.

Reynolds, L. G. *The structure of labor markets.* New York: Harper, 1951.

Robinson, H. A., Connors, R. P., & Robinson, A. Job satisfaction researches of 1963. *Personnel and Guidance Journal,* 1964, *43,* 360-366.

Roe, A. *The psychology of occupations.* New York: Wiley, 1956.

Rothe, H. F. Output rates among butter wrappers: I. Work curves and their stability. *Journal of Applied Psychology,* 1946a, *30,* 199-211.

Rothe, H. F. Output rates among butter wrappers: II. Frequency distributions and an hypothesis regarding the "restriction of output." *Journal of Applied Psychology,* 1946b, *30,* 320-327.

Rothe, H. F. Output rates among machine operators: I. Distributions and their reliability. *Journal of Applied Psychology,* 1947, *31,* 484-489

Rothe, H. F. Output rates among chocolate dippers. *Journal of Applied Psychology,* 1951, *35,* 94-97.

Rusk, H. A. *Rehabilitation medicine.* St. Louis: Mosby, 1958.

Schaffer, R. H. Job satisfaction as related to need satisfaction in work. *Psychological Monographs,* 1953, No. 364.

Scott, I. D. *Manual of advisement and guidance.* Washington: U.S. Government Printing Office, 1945.

Scott, T. B., Dawis, R. V., England, G. W., & Lofquist, L. H. A definition of work adjustment. *Minnesota Studies in Vocational Rehabilitation,* X, 1960.

Severin, D. The predictability of various kinds of criteria. *Personnel Psychology,* 1952, *5,* 93-104.

Sorokin, P. *Social mobility.* New York: Harper, 1927.

Strong, E. K., Jr. *Vocational interests of men and women.* Stanford, California: Stanford University Press, 1943.

Strong, E. K., Jr. *Vocational interests 18 years after college.* Minneapolis: University of Minnesota Press, 1955.

Super, D. E. The structure of work values in relation to status, achievement, interests, and adjustment. *Journal of Applied Psychology,* 1962, *42,* 231-239.

Super, D. E. *Work Values Inventory Form 1.* New York: Teachers College, Columbia University, 1964.

Tilgher, A. *Work: what it has meant to men through the ages.* New York: Harcourt, 1930.

Tyler, L. *Psychology of human differences.* (3rd ed.) New York: Appleton-Century-Crofts, Inc., 1965.

U.S. Department of Labor, Bureau of Employment Security. *Dictionary of occupational titles.* Washington: U.S. Government Printing Office, 1965.

U.S. Department of Labor, Bureau of Employment Security, USES. *Guide to the use of the General Aptitude Test Battery: Section III. Development.* Washington: U.S. Government Printing Office, 1952-1956.

U.S. Department of Labor, Bureau of Employment Security, USES Technical report on standardization of General Aptitude Test Battery. *Technical Report B-381,* July 1958.

U.S. Department of Labor, U.S. Employment Service. *Worker trait requirements for 4000 jobs.* Washington: U.S. Government Printing Office, 1956.

Viteles, M. S. Vocational guidance and job analysis: the psychological viewpoint. *Psych. Clin., 15* (1924), 164.

Viteles, M. S. *Industrial psychology.* New York: Norton, 1932.

Warnken, R. G., & Siess, T. F. The use of the cumulative record in the prediction of behavior. *Personnel and Guidance Journal,* 1965, *44,* 231-237.

Weber, M. *The Protestant ethic and the spirit of capitalism.* New York: Scribner, 1930.

Weiss, D. J., Dawis, R. V., England, G. W., & Lofquist, L. H. An inferential approach to occupational reinforcement. *Minnesota Studies in Vocational Rehabilitation,* XIX, 1965.

Weiss, D. J., Dawis, R. V., England, G. W., & Lofquist, L. H. Construct validation studies of the Minnesota Importance Questionnaire. *Minnesota Studies in Vocational Rehabilitation,* XVIII, 1964. (a)

Weiss, D. J., Dawis, R. V., Lofquist, L. H., & England, G. W. Instrumentation for the Theory of Work Adjustment. *Minnesota Studies in Vocational Rehabilitation,* XXI, 1966.

Weiss, D. J., Dawis, R. V., England, G. W., & Lofquist, L. H. Manual for the Minnesota Satisfaction Questionnaire. *Minnesota Studies in Vocational Rehabilitation,* XXII, 1967.

Weiss, D. J., Dawis, R. V., England, G. W., and Lofquist, L. H. The measurement of vocational needs. *Minnesota Studies in Vocational Rehabilitation,* XVI, 1964. (b)

Weiss, D. J., & Potter, C. S. Electronic data processing and state agency operations. Unpublished study, Work Adjustment Project, University of Minnesota, 1965, mimeographed.

Wernick, R. *They've got your number.* New York: Norton, 1956.

Williams, R. G. *Biochemical individuality, the basis for the genotrophic concept.* New York: Wiley, 1956.

Wolfbein, S. L. *Employment and unemployment in the United States.* Chicago: Science Research Associates, 1964.

Wright, B. A. *Physical disability—a psychological approach.* New York: Harper, 1960.

Index